PRAISE FOR
REPLACEMENT FORMULA

Christine has beautifully crafted a framework that supports, inspires, and pushes other women to stop staying stuck and start creating the life with passion they are meant for. As someone who left my 9-5 and runs a business that I love full time, I know there is no greater gift you can give yourself. I love that Christine has created a manual that not only helps other women believe they can do it but also gives them the specific, actionable steps with which to make the leap. If you're ready to leave that 9-5 and replace your income for good... look no further.

—Lacey Sites, Business Mentor & Success Coach, Founder of *A Lit Up Life*

Perhaps the number one question I get asked as a mindset and marketing expert, is "How do I quit my day job?" How convenient is it that I'll now be able to refer people to *The Income Replacement Formula*? Christine has pulled together the complete blueprint for leaving your job and working full-time as an entrepreneur — a blueprint that includes BOTH mindset and action. Christine is not only passionate, she's also knowledgeable, and in this book, she gives you the roadmap to a freedom that can only come from being in business for yourself. If you're ready to leave the workforce and join the ranks of profitable business owners, then start here. Christine is the mentor that you need on your side."

—Dana Wilde, Bestselling Author of *Train Your Brain* and Host of *The Mind Aware Show*

Christine breaks down the exact steps necessary to leave your 9-5 and start living life on your terms in the simplest and easiest-to-digest ways. She is a true master at her craft of helping women create the business of their dreams. As someone who knows all too well what the journey of breaking free from the chains of a 9-5 looks like, I so wish I'd had this book years ago when I was struggling and stuck. I know it would have simplified the process and I'm so glad to have this guide to recommend to my friends and colleagues going through this journey now.

—Sara Wiles, Online Business Manager, Co-Founder of *The Happy Thoughts Show*

The *Income Replacement Formula* reveals the key requirements to successfully start AND monetize your online business. Christine lays out all of the strategic pieces with her unique feminine voice that is refreshing and inspiring. She combines the stories of her real-life experiences and her clients' experiences to reveal the truth that it's not always polished and pretty, yet, with focus, determination, strategy, proper leadership, AND mindset you can step away from your 9-5 confidently while earning a living from your passion!

—Celia Faye Meisel, Online Business Coach for Creatives, Leaders, and Spiritual Entrepreneurs

THE
INCOME
REPLACEMENT
FORMULA

THE
INCOME
REPLACEMENT
FORMULA

7 Simple Steps To Doing What You Love
&
Making Six Figures From Anywhere

CHRISTINE MCALISTER

Copyright © 2018 Christine McAlister

No part of this publication may be reproduced, or stored in a retrieval system, or transmitted in any form or by any means, electronic, mechanical, recording, photocopying, scanning or otherwise, without express written permission of the author.

For information about permission to reproduce selections from this book, email info@lifewithpassion.com.

ISBN: 9781980851073

Cover Design by Teddi Black
Cover photo by Sarah Hogencamp
Interior layout and design by www.writingnights.org
Book preparation by Chad Robertson
Edited by Deborah Owen

DEDICATION

This book is dedicated to you: the dreamer... the high-achiever... the amazing woman who is ready to create and experience all you're capable of...

CONTENTS

ACKNOWLEDGEMENTS

I have deep gratitude for every single person whose life has been part of the fabric of mine. It's made me the person I am, the person capable of writing and publishing my very own book. If you're reading this, that includes you, and so I thank you.

I also send so much love and thanks to:

Garrett, for believing in me, supporting my big dreams, and always encouraging me to go for it.

My beautiful family, Fiora, Maeve, Mom and Dad, Shannon, Andy and Caleb, Scott, Jennifer and Joe, Nancy and Gary, Linda and Paul, Marilyn and Rodger, Brad and Kim, Nancy and Rodger.

Julie Stevenson for giving so much of your awesome self to do this thing with me from day one.

Lacey Sites for being exactly who and what I needed, and more, from start to finish.

Dana Wilde for helping me realize what this book actually needed to be about.

Debbie Ardan Christian for encouraging me to self-publish.

Brian Goulet for the beautiful pens to write this with.

Deborah Owen, Julie Ann Jones and Nancy Golya for coming alongside me to bring this work to the world.

Sherry Parks, Kalila Bodden, Meryl Lombardi, Nancy Rich-Guiterrez, Cheryl Corcoran, Jamie Johnson, Alli Kelley, Andrea Niño de Guzman, Caitlin Oestreich, Ashley Mondor, Angie Wells, Mallory Mitchell, Donene Taylor, Laura Koschade, Kim Wende, Megan Elias, Megan Stewart, Rachel Neeley, Nicole Dlugosz, Sara Jackson, Meryl Lombardi, Heather Doran, Hannah Von Buskirk, Joanne Murturi, Miranda Tiller, Margaret Stelter, Alayna Weimer, Amanda Thompson, Mark Ramsay, Greg Buia, Amanda Ritchie, Meredith Stacy, Morgan Irish, Caitlyn Saranchak, Jenny Wood, and Dr. Shannyn Pearce, DC, for being key parts of the Life With Passion community.

Mellisa and Stephane Robillard, Joani Livingston, Charlie Hensley, Megan and Jeremy Boone, Brian and Michelle Raney, Nick and Mollie Such, Kathy Milans, Emily Benson, Erin Monaghan, Ariana Sylvester, Sara Wiles, Allison Hardy, David Durham, Lily Nichols, Mollie Fagan, Kim Sutton, Celia Faye Meisel, Jenna Johnson, Mark and Deb Burke, Dr. Danny Heithold MD, Floyd and Ronda Taylor, Gigi Hammond, and Sarah and Matt Hogencamp for the consistent support, friendship and camaraderie.

Marilyn McAlister, Debbie Justice, Kacey Ciresi, Kenzie, and Constance, for taking such loving care of Fiora so that I could write this book.

Jen Sincero for the hilarious inspiration and motivation.

Arianna Huffington, John Lee Dumas, Adrienne Dorison, Arne Giske, Jenny Fenig, Cailen Ascher, Don Hutcheson, Win Charles, David Ralph, Lauren Frontiera, Vix Reitano, Luis Congdon and Kamala Chambers, Marc Guberti, Brendan Alan Barrett, Suzanne Proksa, Dawrance Constant, LeAura and Devani Alderson, Becky Mollenkamp, Parijat Deshpande, Jenny Powers, Matthew Gonzales, Gina Vasquez, Nissar Ahamed, Lisa Schmidt, Belinda Ellsworth, and Megan Hale, for the opportunity to share with the world.

Emily and James Williams, Jessica Caver Lindholm, Selena Soo, Denise Duffield-Thomas, Brad Yates, and Jill Stanton, for showing me what's possible and teaching me how to create it.

And Ray and Nic Driscoll for declaring in a little Guildford pub, "You've got a book in you." You were right, Vicar.

INTRODUCTION

When you were little, you believed everything - anything - was possible. With wide, innocent eyes and a gap-toothed smile, you loudly demanded that you be given all the same opportunities as the big people in the house, whose knees and shoes you knew well from your seat on the floor. Full of determination and desire, you believed you could do whatever you wanted, starting with actually walking across the room by yourself!

It may seem like a small thing now, but to a 13- or 14-month old toddler, it was the entire focus of your day. Until you mastered it, you were obsessed... you never quit, even though you failed, over and over again. You got right back up on your feet, unwilling to give up.

As you got older, you had dreams and goals... big ones. You were going to be famous! Maybe you were going to be a veterinarian, or an actor, or perhaps even president. My choice was to be an astronaut... or work at McDonald's (because I was fascinated with the ordering buttons)... or both.

I'm sure my parents were thrilled with the latter.

Time passed. You got older, and either played by the rules or rebelled against them; more than likely, a bit of both, though you were probably a "good kid." Your world was filled with "practical" voices, telling you what was expected of you. "This is the way the world works", you were told. The young adult version of you, though still idealistic, slowly, sadly, began to believe what the voices said.

Which meant that, along the way, you lost your drive, your purpose. The vision you had for yourself as a child had long since disappeared as you conformed... And you hated it. You got a "normal" job, and settled into your "normal", expected role in life.

Maybe you married the person you were expected to marry, had kids...and tried to convince yourself that was enough, because you were "supposed" to be happy. After all, most of the other people around you were happy, right? Why couldn't you be happy too? Why couldn't you be content with settling for retirement "someday", with having nice things, traveling, and being free from a soul-sucking job....in 40 years?

You didn't see how it would be possible to do something different. Sure, you knew of some people who were following a different path, but when you thought about it for your-self... your fears and doubts held you back. You believed you had to be practical.

But oh! You had such mixed feelings! Jealousy...anxiety

about the future...being overwhelmed... fear...

You feared taking a risk, just as much as you feared fail-ing. And you were especially afraid of what people would think of you either way.

So you hid.

You hid your light under a bushel. You played it safe... while slowly dying inside.

That childhood version of "you" wouldn't even know the adult "you" now ...

Maybe you feel like June Austin, who told me,

> I was working in a full time job for a company that just wasn't thriving anymore. I was comfortable, but I wasn't happy to go to work every day like I used to be. I struggled with self-doubt, fear of fail-ure, and stepping out of my comfort zone. I didn't feel like I could take the knowledge of working as an executive assistant/office manager for 18 years and apply that experience towards my own busi-ness.

Or maybe you feel like Alayna Weimer, a management consultant:

> I was in a holding pattern with my business. It was something I had wanted to do for 10 years, but I felt like an airplane making circles trying to

figure out how to land, unable to see the clear path. I had had a highly successful job with a highly successful company for 18 years and so I felt stuck. Yes, I had 60-80 hour work weeks, but it felt comfortable even if it no longer fulfilled me. My biggest frustration was when I asked myself "what if?". "What if no one liked what I was offering? What if I didn't set up my website right? What if I didn't have the right strategy?"

That all changes for you today, with the book you're holding in your hot little hands.

There has never been a better time in all of history to create a totally new version of yourself. "Now" is the best time to be a woman with the dream of owning your own business, on your own terms. That's exactly why you're here at this time and place, and that's exactly what you're going to learn in these pages.

If you're a high achiever who *knows* you're meant for more than the life you're living right now… but you're afraid there's something wrong with you because you're not reaching your full potential…you're in the right place.

No, you're not doing something wrong. You don't need to be "fixed". You just need to give those big dreams of yours a place to grow.

Welcome, my friend.

You're not alone feeling like a lost soul. The women I

coach all share some version of that story. In fact, it's where I started on this journey too.

I was an honor student, scholarship-winning class president, and most-likely-to-achieve type for my whole young life. I had big dreams and goals, and I knew I wanted to run my own business "one day," but I couldn't see how to get there.

Despite glimpses of greatness - a Telly-award winning documentary that aired on PBS, getting my first horse (a life-long dream) at age 23, and literally being named a Walt Disney Dreamer & Doer (1999) - I felt like I wasn't fully living up to my potential, owning my greatness, shining as the true me.

I knew that, even as a young person, my flame was slowly flickering toward extinguishment in between these momentary rushes of oxygen. So for over a decade of my adult life, I "settled". I felt stuck.

But eventually, I learned that I didn't have to accept the "same old, same old", and neither do you. I learned to light the fire of that small candle of hope, give it oxygen and a place to burn, and turn my life into a blazing fire that not only fuels myself, but that gives light and energy to thousands of women just like you.

I've written this book for you because I know what it's like to be stuck. To be overwhelmed with the uncertainty of what to do next. To be a freaked-out, jealous, cynical, perfectionistic, procrastinating ball of unhappiness sitting on the couch, eating chips and cheese for dinner, trying to pretend your dreams of traveling the world and being famous for something that MATTERS aren't important to you. Oh, and doing this while you still appear to be high-functioning, normal, and pretty happy overall.

My clients get it too.

Mallory Mitchel, the founder of Virtually Mallory, describes,

> I felt as if I didn't know what I wanted out of my life and I was miserable at my 9-5 feeling stuck, with nowhere to turn. I knew I was capable of more but I didn't know what that entailed. I was hesitant to search for another job because I was fearful of the unknown. I knew my full-time job, all the people there, who I needed to go to for different requests, and I was good at what I did. I was allowing myself to just get by because I was able to receive paycheck after paycheck, paying all my bills that I needed to pay, and having funds left over to do some things that I enjoyed. I guess I could say that I liked being needed but I felt like I was drowning in my work on a daily basis. I got to the point that I dreaded going into the office because I knew that piles and piles of paperwork and a never-ending email inbox were waiting for

me. I felt like I could NEVER get caught up with the workload.

In addition to the overwhelm that consumed my day to day life, I also was a HUGE people-pleaser and perfectionist; therefore, I felt like I couldn't leave my job until I had EVERYTHING in order for the next person who would take my position... and there was a part of me that didn't want to inconvenience my boss by leaving. I put on a happy face when I was out with friends, but on the inside I was lost, overwhelmed and desiring a better work life. I didn't know who I was really because I wanted to appeal to everyone and I lost myself along the way."

Meryl Lynn Lombardi, founder of Little Shop of Saddles, says,

I was relocated to Atlanta by the company I work for and had to leave a lucrative part time server job behind in Roanoke. I desperately needed to supplement my income to help care for my horse, pay for her training and advance my breeding business.

I hadn't been able to find a similar part time job in Atlanta and really wanted to do something different.

I also really wanted to have the possibility of leaving my 9-5 while still generating an income.

I had no idea what else I could do and lacked confidence in my ability to do anything other than stay at my 9-5 and be a server. I was stuck. I felt hopeless and sad.

In 2015, I, too, felt stuck, hopeless and sad. I'd just experienced "the sourest lemon that life has to offer," in the words of *This Is Us*'s wise Dr. Katowsky, and yet, that same year, I managed to turn it into something resembling lemonade.

What was that lemon, you ask? The loss of my first daughter, Maeve Evalyn, to a full-term, unexpected stillbirth.

Devastated by her loss, I used the ensuing hurricane of grief to reevaluate absolutely everything in my world... and that reevaluation became the catalyst for me to turn around my unhappy, stressed-out life.

Ironically, by coming out on the other side of that very dark, miserable time in my life, I have rediscovered true joy, passion, and happiness. And I am now privileged to be helping thousands of women around the world do the same.

How will this book help you become one of those rare women who rescues her own dream? Fair warning: *maybe not in the way you think.*

You see, there are probably millions of books available on time management, productivity, and systems and structures. But this book is about the one thing that trumps all of that in the formula for success: *belief in yourself.*

If you're anything like me - and if you're still reading to this point, you probably are - you think you've got to do *everything,* take *all* the actions, keep working *hard,* and trust that *somehow* you can strategize your way out of this pit you've dug for yourself. You believe the lies that you can strategize and "to-do" yourself into success and happiness and freedom.

Sorry (not sorry) to tell you the real truth...and save you the years I wasted...it ain't gonna happen. Let me prove it to you.

I'd like you to take out a piece of paper and a pen (or a new document on your computer) and write out the list of your still-unfulfilled dreams. Things like:

- Having financial freedom
- Having time freedom
- Traveling to all the places you've only seen on Pinterest

- Making a difference
- Feeling in control of your life
- Working when and where you want to, even wearing what you want to wear
- Creating a life you love, that also pays the bills

Now write down what you want to put an end to. Things such as:

- Worrying about money
- Punching someone else's time clock
- Arguing with your significant other about money and/or how you spend your time

Take a look and you're sure to see a huge contrast between the two lists! Which one excites you? Which one energizes you? Which list would you give your life to achieve?

Of course, the list of dreams, not disasters! Those dreams are worth fighting for. They're worth investing your precious time, energy, and even money, in achieving.

The dreams and passions you wrote down in that first list are what make life meaningful. They give you a purpose.

Now here's the good news: I've helped women all over the world achieve their dreams - and more - and end their daily nightmares. I am excited to share with you the simple strategies and proven 7-step formula I have uncovered for believing in yourself, and creating a life that strengthens and invigorates you.

We'll break these down starting in Chapter 3, but here's a little sneak peek for you:

Step 1 - Decision
Step 2 - Mindset
Step 3 - Niche
Step 4 - Offer
Step 5 - Marketing
Step 6 - Visibility
Step 7 - Sales

You're going to learn how to use these 7 simple steps to build your own business and feel amazing about yourself while doing it.

My life's mission is to empower you to believe in yourself with such confidence that no matter what you've been through in the past, no matter what's happening in your life now, and no matter what obstacles may get in your way in the future, not only can you survive, but you can THRIVE.

I'm going to show you how to laser-focus... Because focus combined with simple strategies builds belief in yourself.

And I'm going to share with you my simple, tried-and-true system that allowed me to live true to myself, and quickly start and grow my own successful 6-figure business. Hundreds of other women are using it today to rise above the negativity, challenges of life, and self-doubt to do the same.

If you're ready to chuck all the expectations that have been weighing you down for years, and rediscover the real - possibly hidden - "you" that has been buried under the weight of "shoulds," expectations, and "practicality," it's time to throw off all that deadweight, step out of your own darkness, and into the light, where you can see a clear path ahead of you, one simple step at a time.

I promise that no matter where you are in this moment, and what circumstances surround you, you can work with whatever gifts and abilities you have *right now* in order to create an exciting, joyful, fulfilling, generous life.

I'll also warn you, however, that the first stumbling block most of my clients encounter is self-sabotage. I know you may say, "I'm not doing that!"... because that's what I said too! (Boy, was I wrong...) At that time I didn't even fully understand what the phrase meant. And it's precisely that misunderstanding that makes self-sabotage the most insidious dream-slayer.

To overcome self-sabotage and help you gain the determination you need to achieve your dreams, I'm going to teach you the exact strategies I use with my high-level private clients. By the time we're done, they believe in themselves, own how incredible they really are, celebrate and uncover their true selves, and - often for the first time - gain confidence in their unique superpowers (yes, you have them too!).

Don't take my word for it, though - you can hear it from them! According to Mallory,

After working with Christine, I was able to quit my full-time job and pursue my own business, where I quickly grew my client base to where I had to have a waiting list for my virtual assistant business. Additionally, during my coaching with Christine, I hired an assistant to help me in my business, started looking at turning my business into becoming an Online Business Manager [a strategic high-level operations manager for online entrepreneurs] and increased my rates.

My business has continued to grow as well; I now have two virtual assistants working for me and I've increased my client base to thirteen clients. I would have never expected to have my own business but I could not be happier with how Christine helped to guide me on the path that I am on right now. I didn't even know what I really enjoyed doing until she started to ask me questions. Now I'm on this path that I believe couldn't fit me more!"

Joanne Muturi, Lifestyle Makeover Coach, says,

From the time that I started working with Christine, my confidence has grown, I have exponentially grown in terms of my reach and the people that I am working with, and I was able to raise my prices. A highlight of working with her was my workshops conducted in Nairobi in my home country of Kenya. I had two beautiful workshops which Christine and I worked together to make a success, and I cannot thank her enough.

What can I say, my life has changed very much because I now believe more than ever that I am doing exactly what it is that I was called to do.

To help you begin integrating these same words and lessons into your life, I've created some special bonuses for you; go grab them at lifewithpassion.com/bookbonus.

Now look, I realize we don't really know each other yet, so you may very well be wondering how you can trust me to be your guide on this journey.

All I can say is that I went from being frustrated, depressed, burned-out, and facing the worst loss a person can experience, to feeling vibrant, joyful, and inspired... an unstoppable powerhouse. If I can do it, so can you!

But before you read any further, this is your moment of decision.

I know you've sadly tucked away your dreams in the distant corners of your mind, perhaps allowing yourself to get more cynical, resigned, and critical of others...

I know you're jealous of the people who seem so successful, and you're feeling more and more despair...

You wonder what went wrong… why you're not doing what you love… why you didn't find your life partner, and don't live where your soul feels at home…

You may have been pursuing money as the fix-all, thinking that when you have enough, *then* you'll be happy…

It feels like "someday" you'll be happy, but "someday" always feels just out of reach…

Well if you're ready to change *all* that, and become the most amazing person you were intended to be, I invite you to go on this journey with me. I know you already have what it takes to be an extraordinary person, living an extraordinary life, free from the constraints of a 9 to 5 that drags you down.

But you also have to know that together we'll encounter doubt, grief, fear, and some unexpected bumps. I'll even ask you to go "there"… that place you keep hidden from everyone, even from yourself.

If you're willing to go there, I'll go with you.

You just need to be willing to show up and deal with the fear… because it's so *totally worth it.*

I invite you to do this with me. Do it for your children, or for the next generation of young people in your life. And let's do this for anyone who told you you couldn't, or that it would take forever, or that you are too bossy, crazy, impractical, too…too…too… (fill in the blanks).

Let's do this for anyone who told you you have your head in the clouds and insisted you come back to reality… who told you it's too risky…

If you're a dreamer who believes in yourself, despite everything you're dealing with… if you believe even in just the *possibility* of achieving your dreams…

Then let's do this together. I've heard all these fears and obstacles dozens of times. I've even had those thoughts and internal conversations myself… but I survived and thrived anyway, and so can you. Trust me, when you start to put the pieces together and you actually DO and EXPERIENCE all those things on your dreams list, it feels top-of-the-world, deep-down-in-your-gut amazing!

Finally, even though it sounds cheesy, I want you to do this for *yourself.* Do it for the you who *knows* about all the potential energy stuck inside, waiting to burst out and bloom.

Do it for the you who desperately wants to believe that you were made to do big things, to change the world. You know you're capable of so much more! More visibility, more money, more impact.

I know how ready you are to discover your purpose, your mission, your calling.

It's there for you, my friend.

You're already on the right path.

It's much closer than you think… in fact, it's right in front of you.

So turn the page, and let's get started.

Much love and belief,

Christine

CHAPTER 1
RECONNECT TO YOUR PASSIONS

"Life is an occasion. Rise to it."

– SUZANNE WEYR

For a long time, I felt like I was living a life of drudgery… I'd keep hitting snooze as often as possible, roll out of bed at the last second, rush out the door to work in the dark, already stressed and dreading the day. I'd do my makeup on the 45-minutes-in-heavy-traffic commute, arrive slightly late, and wait for the moment when I could duck out of work slightly early… Then I'd crawl home in rush hour traffic - again in the dark - to let my dog out, work out, eat some leftovers, and collapse on the couch with some Netflix.

Sound familiar?

As I speak with women all over the world, from Kenya to Kalamazoo, they tell me their biggest problem is they feel like they are living without any passion. Their work feels like it is without a purpose that matters to them… there isn't an inspiring reason to go to work… and it exhausts and drains them.

Women like my client Caitlyn Saranchak, who says,

If you're still in a "9 to 5" and wishing you were out… or you're already out but worried you're going to have to go back… I'm sure you can relate to at least some of my experience.

Before I met Christine I was uninspired and life-less inside. I was only existing Monday through Friday to open up and live on the weekends. I was miserable and hated that I was headed toward the same future, written and re-written by the same pen. I wanted to be different. I wanted to change.

I have this creative side that I shoved to the back corner of my mind so the job that paid the bills could take center stage. It wasn't me! I despised my job and used Pinterest to soak up my "9 to 5" woes. I couldn't let it go when I came home, and slumped, bummed-out on the couch. When I did get off the couch, it was to swipe the credit card for a quick hit of happy through online purchases. No one needs that much stuff from Sephora! I felt truly lost.

Or Ashley Mondor, founder of Brave Creative:

Before working with my incredible mentor, Christine, I was stuck in an extremely toxic work environment that left me feeling mentally and emotionally exhausted. I would leave my job feeling bitter and resentful, and like my work didn't matter. I would then bring all of my complaints, frustrations, and negative energy home, which only created more toxicity. I knew I wanted so much more for my life. I craved flexibility, freedom and being able to serve the world with my own gifts, but I didn't know where to start or what my calling was. I just freaking KNEW I needed to break free."

Women like Caitlyn and Ashley are the reason I named my business, "Life With Passion".

When you have passion... a purpose for getting up... excitement for how you spend the vast majority of your time (working)... *that's a life worth living.* It's a life where you aren't just waiting for the days to pass or working for the weekend, but feeling fully alive and fulfilled each day.

Are you in? Great.

If you want to live a life with passion, first you have to be able to identify **what your passions really are.**

Most women actually **know** deep-down what their passions are, but aren't giving themselves permission to believe in them. Often they've left them behind, as if in another life.

Now before you say, "Yeah, I've heard this before, blah blah blah, but it's not possible to make money out of your passions," stick with me, ok?

I don't care if you're an artist who believes you can only be starving... or a woman who loves to help people but struggling in a non-profit job seems like the only solution... or someone whose biggest passion is shopping... this applies to you. We're on a marvelous journey together, starting *now.*

Actually, my own journey started for me - as it does for everyone - when I was a child.

Like most typical 7-year-olds, my passions were crystal clear. These preferences were not taught, but sought. Nature, baby, not nurture. The nurture part is what we're looking at here.

I loved being a leader, teaching or performing for anyone who would listen to me. As the oldest of four, I often made my siblings a captive audience.

I also loved animals, and my greatest animal love was horses. I was determined to find a way to be with horses as much as possible. Unfortunately, although I was horse-crazy from a very young age, my parents just didn't have the money to support a "horse habit."

Around age 12, I earned money for horseback riding lessons by taking over most of the household chores. I got my mom to fire the cleaning lady so I could do all the cleaning myself. I also did pet setting, babysitting, and odd chores like copying my dad's faxes onto regular paper so they wouldn't fade.

Even after years of earning money doing odd jobs, I just couldn't see how it would ever be possible for me to get my own horse; I kept hearing my mom's words in my head, "That's a king's sport."... so in high school and college, *I stuffed down the dream.*

In grad school, circumstances caused that dream to reawaken, and the result, less than a year after paying attention to my heart again, was my very own horse, gifted to me in a way I could never have imagined or planned for myself, but which was the direct result of reconnecting to that lifelong dream. This is what happened...

I was required to create a Master's thesis project, so I decided to make a documentary for the PBS station where I was a work-study student.

After years of stuffing down my "horsey dreams", I took advantage of the opportunity to choose my own topic, and selected a local horse farm. This farm was causing a lot of fuss in the region, and I wanted to see why... while also reconnecting to horses again.

Six months later, I'd created an international award-winning documentary called... (drumroll, please)... "Life With Passion." Yes, that's right. This short documentary that started my adult life, later came back to inspire the name of my dream business.

It was received by the farm with such gratitude that they gave me "Graley," the son of a Supreme Champion stallion and grandson of a Unanimous Scottsdale Champion and US National Reserve Champion.

Graley, who's turned out to be the PERFECT horse for me, came to me because I finally started paying attention to my dreams again, even though they seemed totally unlikely at the time. When I started the documentary, I was a grad school student, living on loans, with no idea of what was next in life... except that I wouldn't be making much right out of school (that turned out to be totally true!).

And yet...when Graley arrived, I had moved to Kentucky, the perfect place to own a horse. Quickly, I found a lovely, completely affordable place to board him and raise him on bluegrass, and the dream became reality.

Thirteen years later, we're still living the dream together, and owning him also started me on my entrepreneurial journey, inspiring me to start my first two businesses: an online marketing company, and an Arabian horse breeding business.

This dream-come-true can be summarized in this way: It happened because I followed my passion.

That's what I want for you too.

Right now, don't worry about all the "how-tos". We'll get there, I promise.

The best way to unearth all your long-hidden dreams and desires is to answer this question: **What were you like when *you* were a child?**

Go ahead... I'm waiting. Take a few moments right now and write down what you just *loved* to do when you were a kid. The activities, the pretend games, the things you saved up to buy, the themed summer camps you went to, the school reports that really excited you, the books or magazines you couldn't wait to read...

Got your list? (Seriously, stop reading and write this down. The rest of the book won't make any sense to you unless you are completely clear on this.)

OK, now that you have a list - and you can keep adding to it as you remember things; sometimes those memories take a while to resurface - think about what it would look like today if you were to realize some of those passions.

Again, don't think about "how" yet; just think about "what".

NOW, THINK ABOUT "WHY"

In order to discover the *lasting motivation* to move forward, you have to know WHY these passions are so important to you.

Anyone who has ever been ultra-successful has been

driven by an internal motivation to keep moving forward with persistence and consistency. When you, too, are consciously aware of what drives you - what serves you, your family, and your calling - you will discover new reserves of possibility and commitment, even when times are tough.

When you're building a passion-based business, you have to find a way to stay on track to a particular goal. You need clarity about why you're building this in the first place.

- More time with your family?
- More time with your animals?
- To surround yourself with beautiful things that inspire you?
- To eat healthy food?
- To have amazing experiences?
- To give back to causes that matter to you?

The business is not the end-all; it's the vehicle or conduit to get you there. It provides you with the means and the tools to have the influence and life you want for yourself, your family, and those whom you serve, both as clients and in the many ways you'll give back when you can, because that's part of your character.

A life with passion.

OK, now take a deep breath and DREAM. Think in the present tense, as if it's already a reality.

What does your dream life look like? What does your

business allow you to do?

Most of the women I work with dream of flexibility and freedom, just like I do. We want to travel a lot. We want to work when we feel most inspired.

There's an important distinction here because lots of times, owning your own business just becomes *you owning your own job!*

We're not getting you free from your "9 to 5" so you can slave away at a computer for MORE hours.

> *"Entrepreneurs: The only people who work 80*
> *hour weeks to avoid working 40 hour weeks."*
> *-LORI GREINER*

Yeah, that's not what we're about here. There are other ways to be an entrepreneur!

For instance, my client Caitlyn wanted to get free of her "9 to 5" so she could spend more time with her husband and show her horses. She wanted to look out the window of her home office onto the pastures where the horses graze, instead of having to travel for hours to train and ride them, and only on the weekends.

After working with me, she did just that, and is now participating in high level riding competitions across the country, free from the constraints of spending her days in a windowless office, eating lunch at her desk, and going home exhausted without any energy for herself or her husband.

She says,

> In my heart and soul I truly believed I was made for something other than the calculator-pushing position I held as an engineer. Sure, it looked good on paper and to my parents, but it didn't hold weight with the dreamer in me. I needed to hear that I wasn't crazy, that I could give up the title for happiness.
>
> Christine became that encouragement, and took my own voice off mute. She honestly became my number one fan! She gave me back what demotivation had stripped away – self-confidence. I had no idea it was missing until I finally woke up with our weekly sessions. Christine gave tough love when it was warranted, or an open ear when I needed a boost back up. She was the prompt to open up my inner dialogue to find I had always had the power in me to start my own business!
>
> And then...I did it. I made it happen! With Christine's help I actually started a business with a full website, email address, social media account – the works! I got paying clients on the books. I stopped impulse spending, stopped avoiding budget conversations with my husband, and as a result, he

and I got together and quickly paid off our debt as well! And...I quit my "9 to 5"!!!!!

Seeing results is one thing.... Well, it's a major thing when you're starting a business, but *feeling* the results is quite another. I get off my client calls feeling completely elated and inspired. I am helping to change their own story. I hear it in my own voice when I tell people what I do. They tell me I light up and that I am actually inspiring them right in that moment. Whoa! I feel empowered and full of potential!

You'll find that when you do work you're gifted to do, and you're passionate about it, you love doing it! Frederick Buechner said,

> *"The place God calls you to is the place where your deep gladness and the world's deep hunger meet."*

Did you catch that? It gets to be about BOTH. Your deep gladness (passion, joy) AND the world's deep hunger. Talk about a win-win!!!!

To help you begin to identify your own "whys", here are some of mine for my business:

- To help as many women as possible believe they can start their own business and do work they love on their own terms, feeling free and creating the life THEY want, like I have

- To travel, so I can see with my own eyes the things I've dreamed about and read about
- To know that I am FREE to follow my intuition and make my own decisions
- To bless my parents for their sacrifices
- To become financially free, not EVER having to worry again about money
- To make my own schedule
- To not be controlled by someone else's agenda or clock
- To pay medical bills for friends and family who get sick
- To live my big dreams and know there was a reason for them all along
- To make a big, tangible difference in other people's lives
- To give away huge, life-changing and life-saving amounts of money to causes that matter to me

These "whys" give my life meaning, which helps me THRIVE.

When you connect to your meaning, you change your outlook on life. You focus on the positive. The possibilities seem endless. Your life changes... dramatically. Because knowing WHY you are committed to your dreams and passions gives you the internal motivation and external energy to get stuff done.

In fact, connecting at a visceral level with your WHY not only transforms your today, it also transforms your future. It helps you understand why you have to put in some extra time at the beginning of launching your business, and it strengthens you when you have to deal with challenges along the way.

Reminding yourself of your WHY every day also subtly shifts your mindset. Instead of seeing perceived obstacles in your way - and trust me, there will be many - you view them as opportunities. Learn to embrace those opportunities as stepping stones, not as stumbling blocks.

Dream of the difference you can make... Dream of the powerful, capable, high-achieving influencer you can be.

To create this transformation, you must first take responsibility for where you are now. Then take responsibility for achieving the dreams you want to share.

So examine your past - your passions and dreams - and apply the lessons to your future. Remind yourself of your WHY every single day, and use that as motivation to make big, exciting things happen in your life, and in the lives of all you meet.

OK, now you probably want to know what to do with all these dreams, goals, and WHYs, right?

Let's talk about that in the next chapter.

And, head over to lifewithpassion.com/bookbonus for a free companion workbook and videos to help you work through the discoveries in this book!

CHAPTER 2
IT'S ALL A CHOICE, AND ONLY YOU CAN MAKE IT

"Attitude, to me, is more important than facts. It is more important than the past, than education, than money, than circumstances, than failure, than successes, than what other people think or say or do. It is more important than appearance, giftedness or skill...The remarkable thing is we have a choice everyday regarding the attitude we will embrace for that day. We cannot change our past... we cannot change the fact that people will act in a certain way.

We cannot change the inevitable. The only thing we can do is play on the one string we have, and that is our attitude. I am convinced that life is 10% what happens to me and 90% of how I react to it."

– CHARLES SWINDOLL

When you're feeling stuck, confused about how to turn your passions and dreams into a business, and uncertain about how to live the life you want, often it's because you struggle to see how you can make a change.

Many people I talk to believe that things happen TO them and they have no control over the results they see in their lives.

I used to think that too. I used to think the exact opposite of what Charles Swindoll said in that quote at the top of the chapter. I thought my life was 90% what happened to me, and only 10% what I did. And I felt really stuck.

When I shifted my perspective, it gave me an incredible sense of power and purpose that I want for you too.

It's time to start training your brain, to believe that your dreams are more powerful than your fears.

Here's an example of how choosing dreams over fears and frustrations colors everyday experiences.

I recently had a mini-physical for life insurance. The agent came to my house to perform a few tests and verify my application.

She was nice enough but was easily flustered, and complained *non-stop* about how she was going to be stuck inside doing payroll - her least favorite thing to do - on such a beautiful day. She told me all about how much she was dreading it, and how awful the day was going to be… blah, blah, blah.

She was in her 50s, and I was sad to see how unhappy this woman was, and how she clearly felt that she was trapped by her job. She couldn't even enjoy the fact that she was out of the office, in the sunshine, with a beautiful view.

It honestly reminded me of how far I've come. A few years ago, that would've been me, joining in, always stressing or obsessing about the next negative thing coming up on my schedule and how I was going to survive it.

> I wasn't enjoying the present because I was too busy dreading what was next... and living in the future put me in a perpetual state of anxiety.

So that meant my **hopes, dreams and thoughts were dependent on things outside my control,** outside the here and now, relegated to "someday..." I didn't realize that they were up to *me* all along!

Here's the key take-away: You are not a victim. (Neither was the insurance lady.) I know that's a loaded word, but I use it with meaning and intention.

Instead, you are a *volunteer.* You have the power to change your circumstances - but you have to CHOOSE to do so.

It can be a little (or very) scary to choose before you know exactly what the next five years are going to look like and how it's all going to work out. But it's also exciting when you realize that you *get* to choose to be open to what comes next.

It could be (and will very likely be!) even better than what you've got now!

I know it feels much easier to play the victim... and to be blunt, that's the choice most people make. That's the norm.

But I ask you: If you've been playing the role of "victim", how's that workin' for ya?

In answer to that question, before you throw this book, or the device you're reading it on, across the room, I want you to know I'm not one of those women whose life (from the outside at least) has been "perfect."

I promised I would tell you more about the lowest lows I've experienced and survived.

The biggie: losing my first daughter, Maeve, to a full-term stillbirth.

Her loss made this 90% / 10% truth really sink in for me. You can see how, in this article that was featured in The *Huffington Post,* on *The Today Show's Parents' Blog,* and on several other outlets:

4 Ways My Stillborn Daughter Gave Me New Life

"The turning point of those who succeed, usually comes at the moment of some crisis, through which they are introduced to their 'other selves.'" -Napoleon Hill

As a long-time high-achieving, motivated, go-getting entrepreneur, I lived for many years under the illusion that life was pretty much in my control.

Then on March 4, 2015, after a perfect pregnancy, my daughter, Maeve Evalyn, was inexplicably stillborn, shattering every paradigm in my mind, with her beautiful, tiny, lifeless body.

In the profound grief that followed, every relationship in my life changed, including the one with my work. I began to re-evaluate what I was choosing for my priorities, and what kind of legacy I would leave, since I no longer had my daughter.

As I set out to make sense of my new, upside-down world, I deeply identified with Napoleon Hill's discussion in *Think & Grow Rich*. He talked about many famous figures such as Charles Dickens, Helen Keller, and Abraham Lincoln, who transmuted the deep grief of personal tragedies into lives of great positive significance.

Over the past two years, I've grabbed life with new determination and passion. I started a new company using my biggest strengths, with the mission to help women know that no matter what they've been through, it's possible not only to survive, but to thrive. And my husband and I co-founded a non-profit to provide support to other families like us.

Here are 4 key lessons that have helped me move forward mindfully:

1. Say "yes" to offers of help

Learning interdependence and accepting help when it was offered saved me. I could not outright ask for help (likely a product of my lifelong insistence on independence), but I could say "yes" to everyone who offered it.

Not long after Maeve's passing, a client of mine wrote a newsletter article on resilience and how it's linked to the strength of your support network. I clung to that newsletter, literally, and to that knowledge in it as, for the first time in my life, I watched myself choose time with people over that extra to-do item.

2. Get vocal

Sharing Maeve's story has fulfilled my desire to ensure she is not forgotten, as well as given permission to feel connected to so many others who have suffered without support. It's true that whatever is personal is universal, and I knew this was my opportunity to be a voice for change.

3. Go back to basics

Re-examining what really gave me life and energy, and giving myself permission to make time for those activities, helped me recover who I am at my core, and move forward from that energy, rather than out of obligation or exhaustion.

4. Stop playing small

That whole "life is short" lesson hit home, and as I drew strength from realizing that I'd survived what psychiatrists classify as one of the worst losses a person can experience, the fear of failure and concerns about what other people think, lost their power. Instead of talking myself out of things, I used that strength to take risks in life and in business, and to enjoy the rewards that came my way.

Above all, I realized I had a choice. As Charles Swindoll said, "I am convinced that life is 10% what happens to me and 90% of how I react to it."

You have that same choice. I invite you to make it and discover the strength on the other side.

So, how do you choose dreams over fears and frustrations?

First, realize that it's not too late. Let's get that out of the way RIGHT. NOW. You're not too old. You woke up today, didn't you? Some people didn't. *How morbid, Christine.* Well, it's true.

My clients aren't only just young dreamers with the majority of their careers ahead of them. In fact, many of the clients I work with are close to the traditional retirement age, starting their second chapter in life, but feeling completely unsure how to do so.

Like Jamie Johnson, a longtime Master Career Counselor and the founder of Paths2Take Consulting:

> Many years ago, I had tried to start my own private practice but some things happened and I ended up going back into the full-time world of higher education. Then, 2017 was a very difficult year. Several major life changes happened within a couple of months of each other including my job of 6 years ending. I was lost. I had no idea what I was to do except start looking for similar jobs.

I, too, allowed myself to be fearful and overwhelmed for YEARS, and chances are you have as well. The worst part is that usually, you *know* you're stuck, but you don't recognize that it's YOU who's keeping you there. I thought if I just kept stressing, pushing, and striving, I'd come across the answer to those frustrations somehow.

The truth is, if I'd known what to do and how to do it, if I could have gotten out of my own way by myself, I would have done it already.

Here's how to find out if you're keeping yourself stuck, too:

Do you tell yourself, "I can't do A because of B, but I can't do B because of A!"? If so, you're keeping yourself stuck in a self-defeating NEVER-ENDING CYCLE! You're **depriving yourself** of the life you are so deeply dreaming of.

Believe me... I know exactly what you're thinking and feeling. In fact, here's what I used to say to myself: "I can't quit my job because I don't have the money from my side business yet, but I don't have time to grow my side business because of my job!"

If you can relate, I want you to know that there's another possibility for how to bring your dream to life.

In fact, there are INFINITE possibilities, but usually, you can't see them yourself because you're just too close to them!

Maybe you need to find someone who can help you see them! My long-time friend, Julie Stevenson, became my right hand woman after she became a stay-at-home mom following the birth of her third and fourth children, a set of twins.

Julie's observation is:

> Christine's super power is seeing all the good, all the talent, and all the possibilities in others that they cannot see for themselves, and asking the right questions and providing the support to help them get there. Anyone who either has big dreams, or WANTS to dream bigger dreams, should know Christine.

So don't worry; this *thang* ain't over yet; not even close. And I'm here for you every step of the way.

What's the next chapter in your book of life? It's the one where the protagonist - the Hero in the Hero's Journey - is ready to cross the threshold. It's when she commits to the journey - the quest - regardless of whatever mysteries lay ahead.

Sure, our Hero still has plenty of adventures - and misadventures - ahead of her, but with the guidance of her mentor, and a lot of perseverance, the reader cheers for her, just like the reader is cheering for you.

I'm sure you've had your share of misadventures, or what you thought at the time were misadventures, too. But I'm also sure you've still had a better life than 99.9% of all the people who've ever lived. My friend Jeremy reminds me of this sometimes (he spends a lot of time thinking deep thoughts while he builds things in his shop).

Jeremy is probably right.

Because here's the ouchy truth: as long as you think it's someone else's fault that you are the way you are - that you're a victim and it's everyone else's fault - you give away your power. Do you really want to do *that*?

On the other hand, you *claim* your power when you realize all those actions that caused you to be where you are today, are either in the past, or out of your control. You can't change either other people or the past, no matter how much you wish you could.

Now pay attention here, this is important: The only thing you can control is YOURSELF, right here and now.

You can control your thoughts, and you can control your actions. That's it. And, whether you believe it or not, that's enough.

So start by being grateful that the challenges of your life didn't finish you off! In fact, you can use the strength you gained from being a survivor, and the story you get to tell about it, to do amazing things.

CHOOSE WHILE YOU HAVE THE CHANCE

Here's a blunt question I feel qualified to ask: **Who has to die for you to give yourself permission to LIVE for yourself?**

I realize that's a shocking question, but it took losing Maeve for me to take charge of my own life, and I don't want you to have to go through anything like that shattering experience. I want you to make the conscious change NOW.

Before we move any further along, please hear me on something. When I talk about your choices in life, I'm not discounting anxiety and depression as real medical conditions. I've been diagnosed with both, my family has a strong history of both, and I have used many traditional, conventional, functional and alternative therapies to treat them. Pharmaceuticals, herbs, supplements, EFT/tapping, psychotherapy, diet, exercise, visualization, testing my neurotransmitters and treating for them, craniosacral massage, inner healing prayer, meditation, journaling, counseling...in the words of Denise Duffield-Thomas, I've "thrown everything at it." And it's all helped at times. I take it seriously because of my own experiences and those of my family's.

But I'm also grateful to report that making empowered choices that led to TAKING ACTION in my own life, has given me great relief as well.

With that admission and recognition out of the way, I also want to point out that *many* people go through their lives filled with regret. Where in your life are you saying, "if only…" right now?

If only I:

- Wasn't with this person
- Hadn't had that thing happen to me
- Didn't marry that person
- Had more money
- Had different parents or family
- Lived somewhere else
- Had chosen a different major, school, job
- Had a better boss
- Had more time
- Had a clear plan

Listen. There IS a clear plan you can follow. You're learning and creating it at this moment. You're here, right where you are, right now, reading this, for a reason. You have no idea what's in front of you... and I mean that in a GOOD way.

"Yesterday is history, tomorrow's a mystery," sings Justin Timberlake. (Several people have been attributed to this quote, but JT sings it best.)

So ask yourself, where will you be a year from today if it's up to someone or something else to make YOUR dreams come true?

I asked this of a client once, and it totally rocked her out of complacency and fear to a place where she was finally ready to accomplish a goal she'd been procrastinating on for nine YEARS!

You don't have to know how it's all going to look now; you just need to decide to **make a choice to take back your power and take control of your life.** That's where it starts. And every day, women just like you are making the choice to be open to changing their own lives.

Now it's time for you to answer this question:

Where in your life have you been waiting for "someday", or playing the victim? Are you willing to change, even if you don't know what it will look like on the other side?

Your life can change really fast when you choose to be in charge, instead of being a victim. It gives your brain more clarity and information about what you DO want, rather than managing and reinforcing all the times you say, "I don't want...", and "I wish...", and "I can't because...." You've been cocooned in those self-protective, self-defeating statements.

When you're honest about what you want from your life, you can move from surviving to thriving, from being a victim to being a volunteer, and it starts with a choice.

Ready to make it?

WHEN YOU'RE AFRAID YOU'LL CHOOSE WRONG

Here's a way to choose YOUR passions and build a business without being overwhelmed by a fear of choosing wrong.

Ask yourself, *What will happen if I don't decide? On anything?*

To decide literally means "to cut off," so it can feel really scary to your brain to cut off seemingly viable options. But, play the (digital) tape all the way through and ask yourself, "Can I get what I want without deciding?"

I'll tell you one thing that EVERY ONE of my clients has done, who has successfully - and permanently - quit their job. **They started by making a CHOICE to believe that it was possible. They believed in themselves, and they believed they COULD do it.**

Like Sherry, the former accounting executive turned wellness coach and founder of Lives In Balance, says,

> While it was hard to dig in and uncover my blocks, I learned I'm no more of a mess than anyone else. I'm just determined to improve because there is no other choice for me. Going back to a "9

to 5″ is out of the question. I feel like giving up and going back would simply be the worst thing that could ever happen to me. So I've learned to dig and look for the clues that lead to change.

Doing these things has built my confidence and really allowed me to see that I am stronger than I think. I'm not the mess I feel like inside my own head. And I can do this!

Are you ready to declare the same? That you're going to stop playing small and you're going to move forward toward your dreams of freedom today?

Because saying "yes" to that choice will lead to everything amazing that awaits you.

CHAPTER 3
UNTYING THE "NOTS"

"Whether you think you can, or you think you can't—you're right."

— HENRY FORD

Andrea was stuck in her job. But she also was stuck in trying to figure out what to do about it. She told me,

I was in charge of creating new businesses for a large food manufacturer as a project manager. While this is a fun job that might sound wonderful to many, I actually hated it. I hated it because I wasn't passionate about finance or about growing a business for someone else. I was working in an

environment where I felt undervalued and unap-
preciated and lived with the constant fear that I
would soon get fired because I wasn't 'good
enough'.

In short, I had a job that I didn't really like, working for people who made me feel like I was no
good. I wanted to coach full-time but didn't have
a clear direction of how to start or whom to target,
and I also had doubts as to whether I was good
enough, or ready enough, to start coaching.

Once you've made a decision to take charge of your life
and your story, and live out your passions, you can then count
on hearing an insidious negative voice in your head chipping
away at your confidence, just like Andrea did.

The closer you get to doing something truly extraordinary, the louder the voice.

You can't really blame it. Its job is to keep you safe, and
as far as your brain is concerned, "safe" means "same". To our
ancestors, safety meant staying within the tribe, blending in,
doing whatever it took to survive, because safety from pred-
ators came from being indistinguishable in a large group. Today, that mechanism still exists in our brains, so it will repeat,
over and over, the same stories you've heard your entire life,
that you don't want to stand out... that you need to be part

of the crowd...

Those stories come both from your own totally natural, fear-based resistance to change, as well as from friends, family members, and acquaintances who allowed their fear of doing something different to keep them stuck in a rut.

The problem is, the more often you repeat those stories to yourself, the more ingrained they become in your neural pathways. In fact, eventually they become so familiar, you think of them as "truth", even if there is no truth in them.

When you challenge the voice and ask, "Why not? Why shouldn't I do this thing that I'm so passionate about?" the voice responds with LOTS of reasons!

Here are some common stories I hear: "**I have big dreams, but...**"

- I don't have anything to offer that people would pay me for
- I'm too old
- I'm too young
- Everyone knows you can't make money in [fill-in-your-blank] industry or [fill-in-your-blank] town
- Someone else is already doing it, and they started before I did
- I'm too far behind
- I always start something and then stop
- I'm scared

- I don't have enough time
- I don't have the money
- I don't know enough/the next steps/how to build a business

Let me state unequivocally right now: NONE of these are valid reasons for not building your own business... even though they regularly prevent people like you from achieving their dreams.

Isn't that a total waste of talent?? I'm really serious about this!

In fact, every one of those stories can be revised as a question that *inspires curiosity*, thereby creating new possibilities as your brain searches for answers to the question.

Let's look, for example, at one of the most "popular" stories I hear: "I don't have anything to offer that people would pay me for."

Revise the statement as a question that inspires curiosity: "I wonder what I have to offer that people will pay me for? I'm so excited to discover it!"

Believe me, you have a *better* story than the ones you've been telling yourself. I encourage you to begin this process. Trust it. And trust that you have a unique gift that a group of people are just *waiting* for you to offer them so they can buy it from you!

Remember this, too: That mission...that vision you have to be of service in the world? *It's not about you.* It's about stepping into your best self to help the people who can only learn from YOU.

Let me tell you more about my client, Sherry, the 6-figure accounting executive. In her prime earning years, she courageously quit a career that had left her derailed and drained, and instead, launched her own wellness business. Now she shares how other burned-out high-achievers can rediscover their own healing and happiness.

If Sherry hadn't discovered her path to express her passion, she wouldn't have been able to show other women how to rediscover their own lives!

AND, she wouldn't have had this amazing transformation, including some surprising areas of her life completely unrelated to business:

> After working with Christine, I have gotten my first paying coaching clients! Wahoo! I've also seen an increase in my essential oil business income by about 30%. While that isn't a lot of money, it is more growth than I saw in the previous two years in the business! And that hasn't even been my primary focus and I'm doing less work on that business than I had been too!

Another tangible result is that I am way more comfortable in my own skin. I have more confidence in my abilities and the value that I offer than I've ever had.

I think that both of these things have contributed to my overall happiness. I feel much more in control now and I know that I have the ability to change whatever I want to change about myself. I can craft for myself whatever kind of life I want. All I have to do is show up for myself.

I've also noticed a difference in my love life. After working with Christine, I not only have men approach me and ask for my number, but I've actually given out my number to men that interest me. Not to age myself, but we are talking decades of neither one of those things happening. And the interesting thing is I am more confident standing firm in what I want for myself and knowing that if the man doesn't agree, I'm going to be okay and not have a meltdown. :-) That's HUGE! Christine and I have not focused on that part of my life at all, but the confidence I have built through working with her has caused men to take notice.

My best friend has also noticed. We don't get to spend much time together anymore as we don't work together like we used to. However, this past Christmas she gave me a gift of a beautiful butterfly pin. She said she knew it was not something I would buy myself or even wear, but when she saw it, she thought of me. She said that she is so proud of me and the work I've done to transform myself into a beautiful butterfly.

How do I feel now? I feel calm and confident that no matter what happens I CAN succeed.

Did you ever consider how flipping the stories you tell yourself on their heads could have a big impact in ALL areas of your life?

The same is true for Caitlyn, the young, successful ladder-climbing engineer who absolutely hated her job! She wouldn't be empowering women through wellness today if she'd listened to the voices who told her to be thankful she had a "good job", and just get over it.

In Caitlyn's words,

To take the next step, you need to know you have the control and ability to do so. Christine helps you realize that inner strength and harness it with tactics that work! There is no doubt you will come

out of your time with Christine refreshed with a
solid business foundation.

I also hear the story (and variations), "I don't know
enough/the next steps/how to build a business."

Turn that into: "I wonder how I can learn more about
building a business? If I get myself mentally ready, I'm sure
the right teacher will appear!"

How much better is that?!?

Remember: "it's not about you". Taking the focus off
yourself and your own doubts and fears will help you come
from a place of service. When you use your unique set of
gifts, others receive the benefit.

Show up as your true self - don't let negative stories hold
you back - and a particular cross-section of the world gets
what it needs from *you*.

Do you know the 1990s Sean Connery film, *Medicine
Man*? The premise is that there is a cure for every disease in
nature.

Similarly, within the greater world community there is a
cure for every need, when you live your passion and move
forward courageously.

In addition, the more money you make as a result of following your joy, the more money you have to give to your
favorite causes, which are different from anyone else's favorite causes. Isn't that beautiful?

Some of my personal causes are:

- Preventing infant deaths, so no one has to go through what I have
- Helping animals
- Supporting orphans & widows
- Empowering female entrepreneurship both directly in my international online community, and in developing countries

What are your favorite causes to support?

WHEN FRIENDS AND FAMILY TRY TO "HELP"

I also want to offer you a word of caution. As you go through this process, you'll get to a point where you're feeling more clear and more empowered. And then you'll tell a loved one about your journey and your dream, and they'll shoot you down.

If you're not careful, you'll end up right back at the beginning, doubting yourself and your dreams, and probably repeating the negative stories again.

This happens to EVERY SINGLE WOMAN I HAVE MET. It happened to me too.

Early in my own journey, while spending time with family, I heard these two conflicting statements come out of the same person's mouth:

"Let's focus on the positives and not the potential problems."

Two hours later:

"Well, for every success story like that, there are thousands of people who didn't make it."

Now, this person meant well, as most family members do. I know she was just trying to help.

But have you ever noticed that no matter how many compliments or positive things people may say about you, it's the negative comments you remember, and ruminate on? That's because, as we discussed earlier, the human brain is biased toward negativity and fear as a survival mechanism.

The truth is, if I hadn't been consciously working on reversing my negative thoughts for the past few years, I would have taken in both of these conflicting messages and been VERY confused.

I've been hearing mixed messages like these my whole life, and you probably have too.

I know I'm not the only one who's been confused by these types of conflicting messages. Your family and friends aren't being malicious; they're just passing on what they've picked up and internalized themselves, believing it as fact.

As a child, you absorbed these contradictory ideas as "truth", even though, logically, they can't both be true at the same time. And trying to reconcile one with the other, you end up in a no-win situation. Now that I'm trained and skilled at recognizing them, I see just how common and damaging they are.

Right now, if you know you're not reaching your full potential, I've got some tough-love-truth for you: if you suffer from self-doubt, lack of belief in your abilities, or fear of failure, I guarantee you've heard and picked up negative beliefs along the way, and those beliefs are winning an all-out, knock-down war over your dreams. *Yikes.*

When you first float the idea of starting your own business, it's very common to get discouraged by what your close friends and family members say. You'll be amazed by how many people express their disapproval, both overtly and covertly. This is because, as you try to create a "new normal" for your life, they become uncomfortable with a "new you".

They don't mean to bring you down, but our society is geared toward people working for someone else, not becoming entrepreneurs. When you want to work for yourself - including taking on the risks of not succeeding - their self-protection warnings start to flash!

"No! Don't be different from the rest of us! You have to remain part of our gang, so we can all complain together! What will you have in common with us if you go off and do this weird thing??" (Kinda reminds you of middle school, doesn't it?)

This is why so many people don't follow their own dream… they follow someone else's expectations.

But you're the only one who has to live with your choices; when you do what someone else wants you to do -

because it makes *them* feel better - you're giving away your power.

"Only take advice from someone you'd trade places with," said author Darren Hardy in his book *The Compound Effect.*

Take a look at the people giving you advice.

Is the person you're asking for advice about your relationships in a happy, healthy, long-term relationship themselves? If not, maybe you'd better find someone else to talk to.

Is the person you're trusting to advise you on your business idea a fantastic, successful, happy, healthy and wealthy entrepreneur? No? They're in a "9 to 5" that they hate, or they don't even work at all? I'd nod my head, say "Thanks very much", and go find someone who's already doing what I want to do.

Cheryl was feeling like a failure and wasn't sure what to do next.

> I knew I wanted to have a business. I had started a few, but was never really able to figure out how to make them successful. I was determined that I could do it by myself because I'm smart, a fast learner, and a good problem solver. That didn't seem to matter. I was enthusiastically going nowhere. I felt like a failure and I wasn't sure what to do next...

> Eventually, I decided to hire Christine because she
> had what I wanted: a successful business she loves
> along with the freedom to work from anywhere.

THAT's taking advice from someone you'd trade places with.

And then there's the person who loves to criticize or complain about everything. Because you know your words reflect your thoughts and feelings, and their complaining proves they aren't very happy with their own life, why would you want to listen to them about yours?

Give them the benefit of the doubt that they're trying to keep you safe. But they aren't exactly qualified to give you advice about starting and growing a business. Right?

In Australia, they call someone who outshines others a "tall poppy," and when we go into self-preservation mode, there's often a desire to cut that unusual poppy down. Even though Americans claim to value individuality and freedom of choice, you'll make a lot of people scared and insecure by wanting to be different. Don't mistake others' jealousy or discomfort about you being unique and starting a business, as genuine concern!

As Robert Tennyson Stevens says in his brilliant book, *Conscious Language*, confidently say to yourself, "Cancel! Clear!" and go find someone who will give you empowering advice.

No one else gets to live your life, so don't let them *tell* you how to live it. Your happiness is determined by what you do with what you experience. You get to choose how you interpret it; as a victim or as a creator. You need to be self-aware and courageous to stick to your dream.

In my case, I had to rediscover my five-year-old self, who was scolded in front of the class and told, "You are NOT the boss of the applesauce!" for trying to lead. I went from being effortlessly confident to a girl - and then a woman - who spent decades as a subdued, meek, quiet, mild, "nice" people-pleaser. Because I'm also sensitive, I was always seeking positive attention in order to avoid uncomfortable conflict and being called "bossy"... or worse.

Embarking on my own journey, starting my own business, now I am fortunate to have people in my life who are comfortable in their own skin and have embraced the changes in mine. My mom describes the change she's witnessed in me as "remarkable".

But many - including some very close to me - have been offended, and have even asked for the "old Christine" back. They grieve the loss of the person they thought they knew... even though that was never the "real" Christine.

Because I am different, I now interact with every person in my life differently than I used to.

So I get it. Many of the women who work with me are afraid of the critical comment, an angry email, or being called a fraud. I know these things are not easy for a sensitive person... they happened to me too. As you learn to live a new kind of life, it's likely your choices will negatively trigger those who knew you "before".

I had to question whether it was worth being the "real" me. I even thought about just giving it all up and doing whatever it might take to restore peace in some of those critical relationships, even at the cost of denying myself.

Fortunately though, when I had reached the end of my ability to handle the frustration, I thought of what Bronnie Ware said in her book, *The Top Five Regrets of the Dying*.

A hospice nurse, Bronnie discovered the number one regret people have when they get to the end of their lives is they didn't live more true to who they really are, instead of who others expected them to be.

You don't need to get to an end-of-life crisis to gain this type of perspective.

Sherry, for example, reports,

> I've been told I'm wasting a "brilliant" mind. My advice is to take it in the spirit it's given. They are likely uncomfortable themselves, and only want what they see as "best" for me. I still love them, but I don't have to listen to advice I didn't solicit.

YES!

The great inspirational speaker, Jim Rohn, said "You are the average of the five people with whom you spend the most time."

So what do you need to do to upgrade your cohort of connections? Can you stop picking up the phone, or responding to emails, or arguing with the person who's trying to convince you to stay as the "old you"? Stop allowing them to "hook" you!

I know their words carry power because you love them and want their approval. But seeking it is giving away YOUR power and dimming your light. And that's the opposite of why you're on this journey.

This doesn't necessarily mean you need to "break up" with all your friends, or immediately kick all the negative family members out of your life.

It does mean it's time to start upgrading your community, maybe even starting with just one new relationship. You could even join my community: https://www.facebook.com/groups/lifewithpassionsociety/, where we have a "no whining" rule! Not because we're Pollyannas, but because we're all there to cheer each other on.

So cry, journal, process, let it go, and upgrade your tribe. Your mission, your calling, and YOU are so worth it.

What will you do today to start taking control of your thoughts and living into your potential?

Thanks to my own struggles to express myself authentically in my business, along with the work I've done with dozens of clients on five continents, I've developed a system *that works every time.*

When my clients apply this system diligently, they get results. Period.

In the rest of this book, we'll go over each of the steps in the system, so you can apply them to your life.

STEP 1 - DECISION

If you are like most of my clients, you are probably what I call "multi-passionate". You're a high achiever with a lot of interests, which is usually good! But for this first step, you must choose ONE of those passions.

The word "decision" literally means "to cut off". You must choose one area of expertise for your business, so you can bring the full force of your focus and attention, which will be necessary to gain life-changing momentum.

So for the next 90 days, pick the ONE passion you're most excited to pursue right now, knowing you can always shift and pivot later if you want to. You'll only gain clarity about this after you get started.

STEP 2 - MINDSET

Think better thoughts. Whether or not you're aware of it - and most people are completely oblivious - you're probably living out someone else's negative thought patterns, imprinted on you when you were a child, and reinforced throughout your life. These include fear and self-doubt - by default - until you intentionally choose to change those thoughts.

The good news is, once you choose to think differently, you are immediately empowered to change your life and business.

STEP 3 - NICHE

It's time to dive in on exactly who you serve and exactly why you are uniquely qualified to serve them! Also called identifying your client avatar, your niche, or your ideal client, we're going to take a unique approach to this critical step that's going to leave you feeling AH-MAZING, too!

STEP 4 - OFFER

The only way you can simultaneously help others while living life on your own terms is to create some premium-priced services that help them strategically solve a pressing problem. This is the path for you to start replacing your income!

STEP 5 - MARKETING

Let's learn to take some simple, aligned actions, daily, on the side of your job or whatever else you have going on in your life right now. There's no need to be overwhelmed, because with this strategy, you're going to be able to let go of FOMO (Fear Of Missing Out) and focus on showing up, connecting, and selling in a way that feels GOOD and doesn't take every single second of your spare time!

STEP 6 - VISIBILITY

When building relationships with potential clients, you must first establish your "know, like, and trust factor". We're going to walk through exactly how to provide the elusive "value" that everyone talks about, so you can build trust, and we're going to get you visible in a way that brings you warm leads who are excited to learn about your awesome services!

STEP 7 - SALES

The word "sales" strikes fear into the heart of many a new entrepreneur, but it's totally possible to sell in a non-icky, non-pushy, non-salesy way! We're talking about trust-based transactions. How good does that feel? When you truly connect with your potential clients with the right attitude and intentions, there's no pressure on either side, and the conversations are natural, exciting, and income-producing!

Let's dive in!

Chapter 4
GET TRACTION ON
YOUR PASSION

"In any moment of decision the best thing you can
do is the right thing; the next best thing you can
do is the wrong thing; and the worst thing you can
do is nothing."

– PRESIDENT THEODORE ROOSEVELT

This is STEP 1 in the *Income Replacement Formula*: Decide. You get to choose your passion.

When faced with circumstances, you have two choices. You can do SOMETHING or you can do NOTHING.

There's no in-between.

Stressing and worrying, day after day, trying to make a decision but feeling freaked out about choosing wrong... is doing nothing.

If you've been doing a whole lot of nothing, it's time to change that. Even if you decide NOT to leave your job to follow your passion... or you decide NOT to do things differently in your business... making a conscious decision allows you to claim your power, which is key to getting what you want.

You're wasting valuable time when you don't make a decision. In fact, "I'm thinking about it" really means "I've decided not to change anything". But you should be aware that there are consequences – some good, some more challenging – for doing nothing.

The original definition of the word "decide" is "to cut off". When you decide something, you literally cut off other options. That's why it feels scary, right? Because you might choose "wrong"?

But when you prune a rose bush, you don't look longingly at the end you've just cut off, wondering what you're missing out on as it falls to the ground.

No, you've already decided that for the BEST HEALTH of your rose bush, it's essential to prune what's unnecessary. Once it's done, your bush will be healthier and fuller, and be able to produce more gorgeous blooms, becoming a better version of the bush you wish it to be.

YOUR FIRST DECISION

The very first thing you must decide is which passion you're going to focus on. Most of us are multi-passionate people and a lot of times, we're kicking around several business ideas or even pursuing a few things at once.

In order to replace your income, though, you've got to decide on just one thing, one passion, to build a business around. And then stick to that passion for at least 90 days without getting distracted, giving up and trying something else, or declaring defeat.

Until you cut away the unnecessary parts of your life and activities that are keeping you spinning in place, you'll never get the TRACTION you need to start moving forward.

The definition of "traction" is "adhesive friction" though "friction" also means "resistance". As I've already pointed out, you'll definitely face some resistance from certain family and friends, but you also can use that same resistance to get a good enough grip to move forward.

So how about it? Are you ready to decide?

Here are some questions to consider as you make your decision:

Which passion feels most exciting to build a business around right now?

What could you spend all day every day talking about?

What's the thing you keep trying to help everyone in your life to be, do or have, whether or not they're actually interested in it?

That's the thing to choose.

Grab your workbook and jot your declaration down there! Put it in writing and make it real.

FOMO

One sure way to avoid getting traction is to allow FOMO (Fear Of Missing Out) to keep your wheels spinning and slipping in place.

In entrepreneurs, FOMO usually looks a lot like "shiny object syndrome", where you feel like you need to try a lot of different strategies, hoping at least *one* of them will work. Deep down, however, you know you're not giving any of them enough of your focused time and attention to succeed, and you never gain the momentum you truly need.

In this case, the opposite of not making a decision is deciding over and over again to try something else.

This constant churn prevents you from being strategic, productive, and consistent.

Andrea Niño de Guzman was there a short time ago. Not only was she in a job she hated, but as she shared with me,

> On top of that I was going into my second year as a single mom and the money I was earning wasn't enough to cover my family's needs. I was looking for a way to not only create another source of in-

come in addition to my full-time job, but also create something around coaching (which is my passion), that could in the short-term become my full-time practice.

I was feeling very frustrated because I felt that I wasn't making any progress in my professional life, mostly because I often became distracted by other shiny business opportunities that would take my focus away from coaching. I also felt that I wasn't ready and that I wasn't good enough to start coaching. I also didn't have a clear idea of what type of coaching I would focus on.

Let's face it; it takes courage to make ONE decision and stick with it long enough to get enough traction to take off. It's understandable that fear might be preventing you from making that one strategic decision.

Maybe you're afraid to:

- choose one business idea to focus on
- pick a way to market it
- choose a package or a price
- invest in yourself to get coaching support
- make the leap and quit your job

It's possible that either FOMO or your fear of choosing

wrong is keeping you stuck, preventing you from growing your dream business.

Let's follow the logic: If you don't decide, you won't actually do ANYTHING, right? Deciding moves you forward. Let's move you forward, so that you, too, can have results like Andrea did, once she decided:

> I am still working with Christine, but so far I have three coaching clients, I have a captive audience who watches me weekly, and I am starting to be known as a coach.

> My success with Christine goes beyond tangible results, because she helped me reprogram several of my limiting beliefs around money and success, and made me feel incredibly comfortable in my own power.

TO-DO LIST PURGATORY

In addition to suffering from FOMO, you may have a (far too) exhaustive to-do list standing in your way.

You're in good company. I've always been a to-do list DORK! Ever since middle school, I have loved my day-timer, to-do list, and checking things off. (You know that thing you do where you realize you just completed a task that wasn't on the list... so you add it to the list even though it's already done, just so you can get the satisfaction of crossing that thing off your list? YEAH. If you do that, you get me now.)

But at some point in my journey, I realized that no matter how much I kept those to-do lists, I still wasn't able to keep on top of everything I wanted to get done.

You see, I was coming at it from the wrong angle. I was approaching it in a way that felt like pressure, and stress, and like all my work was never "enough".

And I burned out over it. I started resenting my business. I started dreaming of the steady paycheck of a "9 to 5" again. WHAT? I know. That's how burned out I was.

So, once I reached fully burned-out/fried-to-a-crisp, I figured it out.

With regard to my to-dos and increased productivity, this one shift I'm about to share changed everything for me.

Think about the reasons all these things are on your to-do list. How does checking things off your to-do list do anything FOR YOU?

That's it! That's the secret! Look at the to-do list and figure out which items actually do something for you – help you achieve your heart's desire – and which are extraneous, just sucking your time like a hungry baby with an empty bottle.

It's one thing if you look at your long to-do list as drudgery. It's something completely different if you shift how you look at it and think about how doing each thing will move you toward your dreams!

Extreme drudgery example: Getting my taxes ready. Ick, who wants to take time to do that (except if you know you're getting a big refund)? So I put it off...

UNLESS you flip it around and look at it as getting your affairs in order, staying legal, proving that you're organized and running a legitimate business, and knowing that you're all properly taken care of. You can lay your head on the pillow and sleep at night because you were honest, above board, and doing something most people are terrified of doing.

See the difference?

Remember that whatever you focus on expands. So focus on WHY you're doing a particular task, not on how much you have to do. Focus on WHY you are doing it, not on the external pressures that cause you to feel like it's a chore or a bore or a nightmare.

STRATEGIC ACTION

"No luck - or anything else worthwhile - will come your way unless you take some form of action."
-T. HARV EKER

OK, are you ready to turn your WHY into strategic action?

Here are the exact tasks to do each day in order to grow your business so you are making money AND saving time. If you focus on these 5 essential daily tasks and nothing else, starting now, you're going to be well on your way to replacing your income and quitting your "9 to 5".

#1 Send Strategic Emails to a Warm Market

I usually communicate with leads and clients via email. When I first got started pitching new business, I began with warm leads. Do you know *specifically* whom you serve with your product or business? If you don't know exactly who your ideal client or niche may be, you shouldn't be advertising. And remember, since you're building a business online, your outreach does not have to be in person! As I said, mine almost never was!

I wrote personalized emails that were very specific to the people I wanted to target and to their businesses, and I explained how I could help them.

Then, remember that the fortune is in the follow-up.

Most people give up after the first contact, feeling frustrated and depressed that the prospect didn't say "yes" immediately. According to online sales expert, Josh Turner it's not until the 9th contact, that you have an 89% chance of closing the sale, so don't give up too quickly! Persistence pays off.

Focus on opening a relationship, not closing a sale. Do this by sending value every time you reach out to your prospect. Try sending an article you either found or wrote yourself, that you think will be valuable to them. When you write back, ask them about specific things they had previously mentioned about how they are doing and what they are working on. Be a PERSON, because people buy from people. Even more, they buy from people they know, like and trust.

After the initial email, I'd reach back out 1-2x per month, because people get busy and also they need time to think about investing thousands of dollars in a service for their business.

#2 Focus and Narrow Your Workload

I only worked on one or two projects of the same type at a time (in my first business, it was creating custom websites). I would sell one site, collect 50% payment upfront, and get to work on it, utilizing one or two key skills (for me, it was writing and producing that website). THAT'S IT!!!!!! You need to put on blinders in order to get traction when you're building your business on the side.

#3 Laser Sharp Targeting

My outreach and follow-up were sent to a specific target market. I wasn't spending a lot of money (actually, I didn't spend any money) on ads or broadcasting to the world without an idea of who I really wanted to serve and how. This is another reason I recommend just offering one or two premium-priced services, which we'll talk about in more detail later. When you do this, you can over-deliver, give your clients lots of attention, and get great results and testimonials to help your business grow even faster.

#4 Keep Track of Your Time

I tracked time so I could identify where I wasn't leveraging it very well. I also wanted to provide myself some accountability to really stay on task, whether I was looking for new business or creating a product. It was also important to me to make sure I had a good idea of how much time these projects were taking so I could adjust future bids to reflect that, if needed.

#5 Consistency Is Queen (and King!)

It is absolutely crucial that you show up in your business consistently. Do these five essential money-making tasks (or your version of them) EVERY DAY. That means every workday, and on weekends if you like (though I strongly advocate for taking off at least one full day every week, in order to recharge your productivity and creativity).

Once you've gotten used to offering your services and you've signed your first couple of clients, then is the time to start looking at systematizing your business; not before.

Please note: the following two daily tasks need to be set up in a particular, efficient order, so you can get the biggest results.

A) Set up Systems As You Go

Once you know what you're offering and to which market, and you've started your outreach campaign, the next business-building task to tackle is setting up an invoicing and project management system. But beware of using this task as a way to feel busy without actually doing the hard work of outreach first!

You need to send an invoice? AWESOME! Now it's time to set up your invoicing software. You need to organize a project you've gotten paid for? PERFECT! Now you can set up your project management system. You can grab my favorite tools for these over at

lifewithpassion.com/bookbonus!

B) Market Organically on Your Favorite Platforms

Finally, NOW it's time for "traditional" marketing: writing your website; setting up one or two social media pages where your prospects already hang out; getting professional photos; designing a logo; creating your brand...

No, this is not the "normal" way of doing things; but you're not building your business to be normal! You're building it with simple strategies, so you can start replacing your income ASAP. *A website doesn't help replace your income. Selling a package to another person does.* When people get on the phone with me to talk about working together, most of them haven't even LOOKED at my website where my packages and prices are clearly stated! They just want to have a conversation, so they can see if they like me and decide if we're a good fit.

So don't waste your time, energy, or money on activities that don't actually *make money*. We're working on YOU and your first offers to a clearly defined audience instead, because that's what works fastest.

Remember, done is better than perfect! You don't have to do all these things at once. You can start with one social media platform, have a friend take your pictures, and upgrade from there.

It's most important right now for you to be focused on getting comfortable connecting with your people, making offers and sales, following up, charging, and delivering.

Remember Ashley, the Brave Creative? She used this strategy and here's what she had to say:

> Christine's helped me show up consistently in my messaging on my favorite platforms so I can connect with clients who can't wait to work with me (which means my following grows daily because my tone and voice resonate!). Christine was there when I landed my first client (without a website, sales funnel or email list might I add!) because she helped me create and refine my offer and messaging.

When Alli and I worked on this for her business, she realized she was focusing her blog on the wrong things.

> Christine helped me change my focus to food blogging while still incorporating farming in a

way that made sense. The branding we worked on for my site is still what I use today, years later, and being so clear on who I am serving has helped me grow my social media accounts in an authentic way, and has led to sponsored content opportunities as well as writing articles for magazines.

She was also able to let go of FOMO and be honest about which platform SHE loved: Instagram. And as a result,

Now my Instagram account is blowing up, my follow-back and engagement rates are WAY above the average, which I have to credit back to Christine! She's a great example of ALWAYS providing value and serving her audience and I've tried to do the same. It is totally working!

Jamie had a different focus, never having marketed her services online before.

I learned I could reach out via social media and share what I am doing. Through posts via LinkedIn and Facebook I started receiving support and interests. I received over 5300 views on LinkedIn alone, from just two posts. I started getting potential clients contacting me.

And Miranda Tiller, a fitness expert, felt a whole new world open up for her:

> After working with Christine, something clicked for me. I felt confident that I could run my business however I wanted to run my business. It's like she gave me permission to make my own rules and do what felt good for me - I didn't have to follow anyone else's rules or use any marketing strategy that didn't feel good for me in my life at the time.

Please note, you should NOT waste your time and energy on the following, because they will prevent you from getting your first paying clients. I see too many women fall into these traps, and I don't want you to be one of them:

1. SPENDING MONEY ON ADVERTISING

You don't know your audience well enough yet. Use your time instead. I know it's limited, but if you're strategic with your outreach, you don't NEED a ton of time to do it.

Maybe you can relate to Andrea, who, while still in a "9 to 5", was trying to do EVERYTHING and do it perfectly:

I am an overachiever and when I started my coaching business I felt overwhelmed by my need for things to be perfect (ie, posting every day, creating meaningful content, managing accounts correctly, having the perfect lead magnet, the perfect page). I felt as if I needed all of my marketing to be done correctly and perfectly in order to have success.

Christine showed me that done is better than perfect, and that I don't need to "hide" behind my marketing. I can just put myself out there, in a warm market that already admires me and start sharing my passion with them. This certainly helped me because I constantly felt that I wasn't doing enough. Today I am confident of my actions, my knowledge, and my ability to grow my business successfully.

See the difference?

2. SPENDING UNPRODUCTIVE TIME ON SOCIAL MEDIA

This can be such a time suck! It can also really distract you from getting things done, and it can completely mess with your mindset because you'll likely start playing the comparison game (and find yourself lacking). Facebook is like a casino; they are both designed to make it hard for you to leave! Reclaim the time and your productivity! If you must check in on social media for some reason other than posting, responding to comments and getting OUT, then set a timer and get out when that timer goes off.

3. SPENDING ENERGY ON LOOKING AT WHAT OTHERS ARE DOING!!!!!

Look, everyone has their own strategy that works, and everyone's at a different stage of business. If you try to take a piece of what this person is doing, and then this person, and that one, you're going to wind up overwhelmed and without momentum. Don't compare your journey to anyone else's. They are all different and that's OK.

We all have the same number of hours in the day...so where can you find yours? For me, it was choosing to do less socially. I'm an introvert, so this worked for me. I LOVED the work I was doing (writing and creating websites about horses), so it made me happy to come home from my job to work on horse sites in the evening and on the weekends. Another place to find more time for your still-new-and-growing business is to use vacation time to travel to see clients (if you need to meet with them in person). It energized me.

WHAT I COULD HAVE DONE DIFFERENTLY TO QUIT MUCH FASTER

If I could go back and do it again, there's one thing I would have changed that would have helped me spend fewer than six years in a "9 to 5", wondering how to get out...

If I were doing it all again, I'd invest time and money in getting help. I would get high-level support and accountability to help me move beyond the employee mindset, so I could more quickly become the entrepreneur and confident CEO of my own business. And I would get help to overcome my procrastination and MAJOR SELF-DOUBT!!!!!!

As I look back at my naive self, I see that I needed someone who would call me out, challenge me, encourage me, AND show me, step-by-step, exactly how she had done it all herself.

Now, that's what I do for my clients, like amazing Ashley:

> Christine shows up from such a loving and intuitive place and because of that, you not only look forward to every single call/email/Facebook post but you know you're going to take huge steps forward towards your business' success! The hardest part as a new entrepreneur is investing in yourself and your dreams. Working with Christine has

been the best investment I've ever made and you
owe it to yourself to make your dreams a priority!

I want that for you, too. I want to help you take the
shortcut to your destination. Think about it: What's it worth
to you getting to spend more years of your life doing what
you love, rather than what drains you?

You can start here: lifewithpassion.com/bookbonus

CHAPTER 5
MINDSET ISN'T THE MOST IMPORTANT THING...
IT'S THE ONLY THING

"Success is between the temples."

— UNKNOWN

This is STEP 2 in the *Income Replacement Formula*: Mindset. It's so important, I've included multiple chapters on different aspects of mindset, each of which is critical to your success.

I know you're ready to replace your income and quit your job... or never have to go back to it. But since it's so scary to do it yourself, maybe you've wished – or even prayed – that some outside event would cause you to have to leave.

If you're like me and many of my clients, you've had a loop in your head going for years now. **You've even felt desperate at times,** wishing for a layoff (so you could collect unemployment and use that safety net to grow your business) or maybe even something more drastic, like a hospital stay. *Anything* to prevent you from having to show up every single day to a soul-sucking job.

Maybe you're looking around at other people who have successfully quit and you're wondering, "Why can't I do that too? What's wrong with me?"

And now, in this book, you've reached the point where you've rediscovered your passions, you've made a choice about whom you want to serve, and you're even acutely aware of all the "why not" reasons you've been fed your entire life... and you're changing that diet of negativity for one of possibility.

What's next?

Now it's time to take a look at the stories you're telling *yourself.* The ones other people give you are much easier to identify. But the stories you tell yourself are the ones that matter MOST, because they fall within the 90% of things you CAN control: your attitude about the 10% of what happens to you, like that great quote in Chapter 2, right?

Maybe you have a list of "reasons" why you can't quit:

- "I need that steady income."
- "I need the benefits and the health insurance."
- "I have a family to support."
- "I don't have the right degree."
- "No one wants to pay for what I'm selling in my town/state/country."
- "I might fail spectacularly."
- "I don't know what I would do instead."
- "It's not practical."
- "I'm scared." (note: this is the biggest reason most people don't leave, whether they realize it or not)

You're soooooo not alone. Here's what Alli Kelley, who came to me a work-at-home mom with a big dream of going full-time with LongbournFarm.com, said:

> Before working with Christine, I lacked confidence and a positive mindset about my business, my abilities to make it successful, and my choice to be self-employed via a blog. I felt frustrated and hopeless. I didn't know where to look for answers in my business.
>
> The most important thing Christine did for me was help me change my mindset. She taught me

how to have a positive approach to ANY problem and how to have an abundance mindset. This training has served me again and again and again.

I don't get distracted like a lot of others in my niche; I am able to stay focused on my goals instead of being blown about by a competitive mindset or fear due to algorithm changes, or anything else. I have actually been asked by other bloggers how I can be so calm when big changes happen or when I think about competition. I briefly share what Christine taught me every time and pass credit to her!

Alli quit her job while we worked together and now she's able to run her dream business, all while being more available for her family - which includes two young children – and her farm.

Here's what I want you to know:

MINDSET IS (ALMOST) EVERYTHING

If there's one thing I didn't give enough weight to when I started my first 3 businesses, it was mindset. I had no idea I should even pay attention to it. Instead, I simply set goals, checked off stuff on a to-do list, got stuff done, and made some money.

But I also had these phrases on automatic repeat in my mind:

- I don't know what I'm doing wrong.
- Everyone else seems to be succeeding, making more money, but not me.
- There has to be a better way, but I just can't seem to find it.
- What's wrong with me?

Both when I was in my "9 to 5", wishing for a way out, and when I was running a booked-out online marketing business, I was feeling stressed, stuck, and alone.

What was the common denominator, despite wildly different ways of spending my days and making my income?

My mindset.

Self-doubt was creeping in, and I felt heavy and sad, and I didn't know what to do about it.

At first I knew I was frustrated with a job I didn't want to be in, and then later, with a long-standing income plateau in my online marketing business... and I was close to burnout with how hard I always seemed to be working.

I looked around at people who were having more fun while making a whole lot more money, and I thought, "What do they know that I don't?"

I decided to hire one of them to help me figure that out. Even giving myself permission to pay someone to help me was a big deal, because for so long I'd been telling myself I SHOULD be able to figure it out on my own, for FREE.

But as long as I kept trying to do that, I kept getting the same results: staying STUCK. *Everything changed when I hired someone to bust me on my stubborn, self-sabotaging beliefs and teach me how to replace them with more empowering thoughts and beliefs.*

I learned to speak in the language of possibility. I started to dream again... And dream big. Then I saw those dreams start coming to life... quickly. Five years earlier I'd printed out images of a trip to Italy, and a dream house, and kept them by my bedside. Now they were really happening, within just five months of hiring my first coach!

I encourage you to give yourself permission to dream big too. To speak the language of possibility, and to get someone to bust you on *your* stubborn, self-sabotaging beliefs. It's like giving your brain a breath of fresh air, instead of the stale, recycled air it's been living on all these years.

More important even than developing strategy and taking action, is retraining your brain to default to self-belief instead of to sneaky self-sabotage.

Want proof?

Within three weeks of hiring my first mentor, my income tripled. Tripled!

Why?

No matter how capable I thought I was, I needed someone to help me spot and fix the areas and blind spots that I just hadn't been able to see on my own.

I believe every person has some area of expertise and an important message to share. That's why you're here, right?

So what's holding you back? Is it the same thing that's been holding you back for a while? (Hint: Probably).

You already know what you need to know and you're already capable of sharing it right now. You're a high-achiever, after all! If you find yourself procrastinating or not following through… if you're not executing… if you don't have the results you want… if you're overwhelmed, freaked out about visibility, scared of failure…chances are good that it's a mindset issue.

Maybe, like Caitlin Oesterich, owner of Savvy Cowgirl, you've already started your own business, but you're struggling. Caitlin says,

> Before working with Christine, my new business was chaotic, unfocused, and draining, both financially and emotionally. I had been trying to make a business out of Savvy Cowgirl for over a year and wasn't experiencing any growth. In fact, my business was costing me so much money I was having to supplement it with income from my "9 to 5" and was seriously considering throwing in the towel. I didn't want to give up on my business,

but I knew that if I couldn't find a way to make some money, I would be forced to let it go.

The GOOD news is that you can turn this around and discover confidence and clarity about your business, and the path will become clear, like it did for Caitlin:

Soon after starting to work with Christine, I had my first profitable months in two years. Not only that, but I sold out my entire group program and doubled the amount of people that I originally planned for the program.

Suddenly, I was being approached by other business owners to collaborate on projects, and new potential clients were seeking me out locally for help with their ranches. My family has started asking me how they can make money doing what they love as well now too.

I no longer feel unsure if I should continue my entrepreneurial journey because I know that I have the tools necessary to run a successful business.

Christine's service is for any female entrepreneur that has been spinning her wheels, stuck in a "9 to

5″, and lacking the confidence to change her business from a hobby to a profitable, legitimate business. When you work with Christine, you gain the clarity and confidence you need to be in the right mindset to build a successful and profitable business. More, Christine has real world experience and strategies to grow your business from the ground up.

And those, my friend, are the exact same strategies you're learning in this very book.

I've seen it time and time and time again with my clients. If you're not happy, content, at peace, or joyful on the inside, the coolest trip or experience isn't going to be meaningful, and you're still going to be stuck – mentally and even geographically! – right where you are.

Your outer world is simply a reflection of your inner world, and when that inner world is stressed, chaotic, or unclear, the same filters get applied to the outer world. It doesn't matter whether you're sitting in a miserable, fluorescent-lit cubicle, a home office, or in a gorgeous hotel in Paris, if you don't clear up your inner world, your outer world will never feel quite right.

Instead of telling yourself you're "too busy" with all the to-dos and strategy planning – all the external things like newsletters, articles, ads, etc. – you need to make time and space to do the inner work.

If you're like most high-achievers, it's going to feel completely unnatural at first. You will resist it and feel that it's a waste of time with all of your action-oriented being. But it's not. It's critical.

In my own journey, as I began to do this mindset work, I noticed that I became much happier, and I felt more settled; I enjoyed whatever I was doing more. I also noticed that great clients started seeking me out, and my business became a joy.

I realized I'd had a fear of not being busy, that if I weren't constantly working on my business, it wouldn't grow; I'd carried that belief over from my previous business. I could see it wasn't serving me though, as my audience grew to thousands and I worked with more clients than ever before.

Sometimes my clients wonder why I focus so much on the internal work. This is why: because no matter what sorts of external systems and structures you put in place, if you're not feeling clear, confident and energized about your business, you're not going to show up as powerful and you won't be able to serve your clients.

It's the opposite of how you THINK it works when you first start a business. You think you have to focus on all the external stuff and just get going. But you actually have to START with mindset.

Have you been feeling unclear about your goals or desires? Do you wish you had more confidence? Have you been putting off doing this critical mindset work? If so, follow these exercises, so that you, too, can feel like Alayna:

> I felt like I was unable to truly enjoy the life I had
> created up to this point [starting her business]. Af-
> ter working with Christine, I realized that I have
> the ability to create the life I want.

If you want to get out of your job so you can create and run the business you're passionate about, full-time, two simple questions can change how you think, and therefore, the actions you take.

#1 "WHAT IF IT IS POSSIBLE?"

Instead of saying, "I wish I could quit my job!", "THAT would be nice," or "She must have some advantage I don't have", start asking yourself, "What if it IS just as possible for me?"

What if those other business owners aren't lucky or special, but they started to ask themselves how to *make* it possible, and then they found the answer to their own questions?

What if, like TONY ROBBINS says, they "ask better questions, and as a result, they get better answers"?

It all starts with you believing it's possible and getting yourself in the driver's seat. Stop looking for all the reasons starting your business is NOT possible!

MINDSET IS ABOUT BECOMING THE WOMAN WHO BELIEVES IN HERSELF

It's about understanding that your thoughts and words literally create the reality you experience every day, and that they can be changed. As you change the thoughts you think and the words you speak, your reality changes too!

Remember that I told you we'd get to the "hows" of your business? Well, THIS is the foundation on which all of the "practical strategies" rest.

It is not about having any one perfect marketing strategy or website. You grow into those things. It is about starting with what you have right now, believing in yourself, and taking action out from that place.

THEN you, too, will discover what my client Morgan Irish did:

> Christine is perfect for women who are looking for permission to be their best selves. We are capable of so much, yet often just need the validation to take the first step. And Christine not only takes the first step with you, but the second, the third, and continues as long as you allow her the opportunity. The result of time spent with Christine begins with empowerment, and if followed through, ends with a carefully crafted plan and execution

of the goals and dreams formerly thought of as distant.

In his book, *The 10x Rule*, Grant Cardone states that you must be willing to **commit first, and figure out how to make it happen along the way.** The author argues that commitment, NOT having the right plan or knowing all of the "hows" before you start, is the key ingredient in success. **Commitment.**

It doesn't require any money, any time, any degrees or programs; it's a choice that only YOU are capable of making and sticking with.

So often, as women, we feel the need to do exactly the opposite; to plan, to prepare, to work on lowering risk, to look at all the reasons things might or might not work out. We get caught up in our stories (or the stories of those close to us) of how things haven't worked out in the past or why now isn't the right time or why our dreams aren't practical… and we once again resign ourselves, with a sigh, to staying practical, safe, and waiting for "someday".

Those dreams you have are yours for a reason. So I have a question for you:

ARE YOU COMMITTED?

Are you the kind of woman who sticks to things once she decides she's going for them, or do you discover reasons why something isn't a great idea when you hit resistance or challenges along the way?

Maybe you feel like you've tried your best and haven't seen the movement or success you want in your business yet. Maybe you've come up against some circumstances or obstacles that have really derailed your progress.

The good news: you can still commit, TODAY, to seeing your dreams through.

On the heels of opening yourself up to that possibility is the next, more practical question:

#2 "How can I?"

(Yes, we're finally getting to the "how". Are you so excited?!?!)

So, if you're starting to believe that it's possible for you, too, then how could you make that work? What would that look like first? Then what would be next?

You can grab my [opt-in - how to escape your "9 to 5"?], join my free community, or maybe your next step is to set up an in-person or virtual coffee date with a successful entrepreneur whom you admire, and ask them how to get started.

Almost every single successful entrepreneur has had someone help them along the way. So identify someone who inspires you, connect with them in a very helpful way, and over time, see if you can engage them in conversation. If you hit it off, you may be able to take them out for coffee, or offer to help with some introductions that would be helpful to them, or hire them to help you if they're available. In the process, learn what you can from someone who's actually doing the kind of things you want to do.

No matter what your next step is, **these questions are about training your brain** - which has been mired in an employee mindset, always looking for certainty, afraid to take a risk - so you can start looking for possibilities, which is integral to the entrepreneur's mindset.

Change your inner narrative with these two simple questions, and your behavior will shift, too.

No more, "Must be nice for them!" Now it's time to start asking yourself, "What if it's possible for me too?"

BELIEVE that it is, indeed possible, and then get curious: "How can I do this too?" **And watch what opens up for you.**

So we have these two powerful questions, and they're an awesome start, but what's next?

It's time to notice the way you speak to yourself AND to others, and be willing to change it.

IT'S TIME TO UPGRADE YOUR LANGUAGE

Upgrading your language, phrase by phrase, is a very tangible, simple, and free way to change your thoughts and feelings. It helps you say things that are actually in alignment with what you desire for your life. It might seem too simple to be useful, but it's super-smart and powerful.

You might be wondering what this looks like in practice.

1. SAY "WHEN," NOT "IF."

I've talked to some women who say they want to change their lives, but are full of reasons why they need to wait, or why it might not happen, or what they're going to do IF it doesn't work.

The most successful people are ALWAYS the ones who say "when," not "if."

That small change in your vocabulary could be the start of a whole new outlook on your life!

I LOVE this quote from Jen Sincero in her book, *You Are A Badass* (published by Simon & Schuster):

> *"It was about no longer being the person who takes what she can get, but finally being the person who CREATES what she wants."*

How confident are you that you're creating what you want? Are you feeling stressed, anxious, or uncertain?

YOU ARE CAPABLE OF LIVING UP TO YOUR EXPECTATIONS FOR YOURSELF.

You don't have to know it all before you get started (no one actually EVER does!).

So start by saying "when," not "if."

My client, Mallory, was all about strategy when she came to me, admitting,

> "I will say that the mindset work was one of the hardest parts for me. But Christine is able to break things down into simple and manageable practices and tips that really helped me start to break away the negativity that had been built up in my mind for so long. She really did help me breathe belief back into myself that I was capable of doing WHATEVER I wanted in life. She also helped me give myself permission to dream again."

And now, she has a booked-out business, multiple team members and a waiting list of clients who can't wait to work with her!

The words you speak have a direct impact on the results you see in your business, bank account, and life.

So, which words do you regularly use when you talk to yourself?

2. ELIMINATE "I CAN'T."

You know I'm all about simple strategies, so let's start by replacing some of the most damaging words I hear people say - "I CAN'T."

Have you ever found yourself saying something that starts with "I CAN'T?"

- I can't quit my job because...
- I can't seem to get clients...
- I just can't seem to replace my income...
- I can't figure out what I'm doing wrong...
- I can't focus...
- I can't seem to stop procrastinating...
- I can't find enough time to do what I want to do...

Ahem, I used to say ALL THOSE PHRASES MY-SELF, so I'm raising my hand right alongside you, but here's the thing...by saying those words, you are actually affirming they are true and perpetuating them into the future!

Instead, replace them with

- I AM moving toward quitting my job
- I AM getting clients
- I already HAVE all the pieces to move forward
- I CREATE the time to focus today
- I DO have the ability to move forward today

This isn't just "woo-woo"; it's neuroscience. You have neural pathways that make the habitual "I can'ts" feel familiar and "true". The new phrases feel unfamiliar and false at first. The cool thing is, your brain looks for reasons to confirm whatever you believe/think/speak is TRUE.

So, when you speak, you are actually affirming and

creating more of what you said, so let's change what you say to something in line with your true desires and values!

So the next time you find yourself saying, "I can't...", how will you replace it?

3. BANISH THE BIG, BAD "I DON'T".

"I don't know how" is probably the common way this busted phrase shows up, but of course there are others, so start to notice which ones you use!

To upgrade right now, transform "I **don't know how**" into...

"How can I...?"

Like my client Laura, who very quickly found a way to quit her "9 to 5" when she stopped saying "I don't know how" and instead asked, "How can I?"

After years of wanting to quit, but full of uncertainty about if, when, or should she, Laura decided to be open to making a plan. We spent a focused day creating her first packages, pricing and messaging, and ended the day with a "coming out" livestream where she shared with my community what she'd created and what she now had to offer them.

Within four weeks of that day, Laura handed in her notice at her job.

Why? Because she moved past spinning the story of "I don't know how," decided to be open to possibilities, figured out the first steps in the "how", and then just did it.

If you give your brain the chance to look for the answer in the background of the rest of your life, it will! The answer might come to you while you're showering (that's why I love Aqua Notes!!! http://bit.ly/aquanotes-notepad), washing dishes, or driving (you can create a voice memo on your phone to capture it!).

Here's a quick reference guide of other no-no words, and what to upgrade them to:

- I DON'T KNOW - ->I CHOOSE TO KNOW
- I CAN'T - ->I CAN
- I'M NOT - ->I AM
- I WON'T - ->I WILL
- I WISH - ->I CREATE
- I'M TRYING - ->I'M DOING
- I HAVE TO - - > I GET TO

All these phrases are POWERFUL, but you get to decide which side of the chart you're using - one to make things easier for yourself, or the more challenging side.

Upgrade the way you TALK - and it will require you to upgrade the way you think! If you've ever struggled to change your thinking, this is an awesome, very practical way to back into it!

Which of the "before" phrases do you catch yourself saying a lot? Which ones are you committed to upgrading to the "after" phrases? Start upgrading right now!

I found the book *Conscious Language* by Robert Tennyson Stevens to be extremely powerful (and cerebral!), and he gives many more examples just like those above.

4. GET AN ATT-I-TUDE OF GRATITUDE

Changing your language to an "attitude of gratitude" teaches your brain to look for all the things going right.

Your brain is designed to pick out the negative (that one comment you got on Facebook when all of the others were positive; the one time you got a B; the one area that "needs improvement" on your job review). This is an ancient mechanism from when humans were often prey. Your brain is designed to notice what's different in your environment, and alert you that it might be a tiger waiting to eat you. Seriously.

While these negative experiences and perceived threats are not actual life-and-death circumstances anymore, your brain reacts as if they are. Remember the whole "safe is same" thing? Even if it makes NO sense from the outside, even if everyone around you can see how capable you are of creating your dreams, you might be holding yourself back because of the potential negatives.

Gratitude is a word you hear a LOT in the personal development world, and for good reason (remember when Oprah made "gratitude journal" famous?).

Gratitude is TRANSFORMATIONAL for your life and business. If you haven't yet experienced or come to believe that, then stick with me, because this has the power to be life-changing for you. If you already agree, stick with me too, and anchor it in more deeply.

Gratitude has the power to totally turn your day around. It's one of the "highest" emotions on the scale, like joy.

I used to think it couldn't be that easy; it has to be more complicated than that, right? But once I tried it, it was like how I felt when I quit my "9 to 5": what took me so long?

Now gratitude is a non-negotiable part of my daily morning ritual, and I can tell a tangible difference in my mindset if I skip it. Writing down 10 things I'm thankful for moves me up from "blah" or anxious or confused or frustrated or overwhelmed, to a state of being much clearer, calmer, and happier.

Often, when I'm working with clients who are in one of the lower emotional states, implementing this simple ritual yields nearly instant positive results in their life and business. There is no magic pill to make you an overnight business success (and anyone who says there is, is lying :)), but practicing gratitude is one of the closest things to a "happy pill" I've ever found.

Gratitude changes your state of mind so you can make wiser decisions for your business and you can more clearly see what's working. That, then, helps you identify those all-important money-making tasks that savvy entrepreneurs focus on almost exclusively (especially in the beginning of their business) so you can follow through and make money!!!

Gratitude actually gives you a "better brain," because it takes your brain out of stress – "how will it work, what if it doesn't work, I'm scared that it won't work, I'm so stressed" – and moves it into POSSIBILITY. It puts that powerful brain of yours to work in a much more productive way.

When I approach my day full of gratitude, I come into it focused on what IS working and I EXPECT more good things to come, and then guess what? They do! I know that might sound crazy, but it works! And, what do you have to lose by trying it?

What about you? What are you grateful for?

5. TRUST THAT EVERYTHING IS HAPPENING FOR YOU

Byron Katie wisely said, "Everything happens for you, not to you."

Have you ever thought about that before? If not, consider what it really means. The implications are huge.

If someone says to you, "You look tired today", you could give it a variety of meanings: "You look terrible." "You are working too hard." "I'm glad I look better than you do." "I'm worried about you."

Do you see how your response will change, depending on the meaning you give to their statement?

Here's a personal example. One Sunday, after a large amount of effort, planning and time investment, I made it to the barn but didn't get to ride Graley as planned. It started raining the minute I put his saddle on. Instead, of getting upset about the rain and my canceled plans, I chose to change what the rain might mean for how I spent my time. I got to practice with him on something he really needed to practice, which I would not have taken the time to do otherwise.

I also discovered on that trip that one of my horses was having a hoof issue. I was able to go back later on to get it checked out, and I was fortunate to get another chance to ride in the process. Instead of being upset, I looked for what else the rain could mean to my day.

There have been SO many times in business where I was initially disappointed because I was really attached to a certain outcome, and then years later, I found out that it was such a great thing.

Here's just one example: Many times, I got really excited about working with a potential client, only to have them drop off the face of the earth. When I was in online marketing, more than one of these potential clients wound up filing bankruptcy and leaving many of their vendors unpaid. BULLET DODGED!!!!!

As a coach, I've cultivated the belief that ideal clients come to me at the right time instead of feeling like I have to "get" them to do something to work with me. Because I have chosen that belief, it supports me in feeling calm, clear and grounded, trusting that there is ALWAYS a greater reason why, even if I don't understand it today.

You've probably had experiences like this too, where you

can look back with gratitude that something you REALLY wanted at the time didn't happen, and now you can see why. What were those times?

And what have you learned on your journey that you will carry to make this new adventure a success?

You now have at your fingertips a whole new set of proven techniques to begin upgrading your mindset, the reality you experience, and your results, right away.

Where will you start?

Make sure to grab your companion workbook over at lifewithpassion.com/bookbonus and work through this chapter's questions to help you lay a strong mindset foundation even faster!

CHAPTER 6
SHOW ME THE
MONEYYYYYYYYY!

"What we really want to do is what we are really

meant to do. When we do what we are meant to

do, money comes to us, doors open for us, we feel

useful, and the work we do feels like play to us."

– JULIA CAMERON

MONEY

That word caused me major anxiety and stress for most of my life (tense shoulders, stomach pain, fight-or-flight mode symptoms).

So before we dive in and talk about exactly how you're going to MAKE the money to replace your income... so you can quit or stay out of your job... I first want to ask...

How do you feel about money?

When I first became a business coach, I was shocked to learn that our beliefs about money (our "money stories") are set for us by the time we're eight years old.

Early in my life, I picked up the belief that there was never enough money to go around. No matter how much money I made, this long-held belief held me back from taking risks, and prevented me from getting to the next income level... for years. From the time I left my "9 to 5" and replaced my income during the first month in my own business, to the time when I finally felt like I was a proven, successful entrepreneur, I still believed deep down that there was a finite, small amount of money available for me.

Even if you aren't aware of it, you have deeply held beliefs about money too, which come from the influence and impact of others. More than likely, you're living out *someone else's* "money story"; usually that of a parent, grandparent, or someone else close to you when you were young.

To help you identify *your* money story, let me share how I struggled with my own endless loops regarding money:

- **There's never enough.** For many years, even if something amazing happened with money or I accomplished a big goal, I'd revel in it for a hot minute, then immediately feel anxiety about where that money needed to go, and where the next chunk was going to come from.
- **The only way to make more money is to work more**

hours. I would think: How can I do that? I already work all the time. I must not be doing the right things... I'm not doing enough... I'm not efficient enough.... It seems like the only way to get enough money is to just buckle down and find a way to spend MORE hours working and obsessing about finding more work. And I SHOULD be able to figure it out for free (by reading books, articles, downloading free-bies, etc.) because I'm smart and independent and running a profitable business.

- **Spending money on anything but practical stuff is bad and I should feel guilty about it.** So buying myself clothes or shoes, eating out, getting a pedicure or massage, or anything not basic and "practical" would cause major guilt. "Treat yo' self" was a foreign concept reserved for people on TV.

Does any of this sound familiar to you? It's painful, isn't it? Here are some more negative money thoughts:

- Making money is hard.
- Focusing on making a lot of money means you have to give up something more important, like time with your family.
- You have champagne taste on a beer budget, and that's a bad thing.

- It's wrong to buy nice things or spend money on impractical things for yourself.
- You should only buy something if it's on sale.
- Horses are a king's sport and not for us commoners.
- Your friends' families have a lot more money than you do.
- You have to make decisions - you can't have it all.
- Debt is shameful and you're wrong if you have it.
- You can have nice things someday... when you retire... maybe.

And, this one especially plagued me:

"THIS CAN'T BE WHAT I'VE BEEN WORKING SO HARD FOR. IT JUST CAN'T."

This is exactly what I used to think.

I felt like there was something wrong with me, that I wasn't doing "it" right, because I wasn't making the kind of money I really wanted, but I didn't know what else to do! What was I missing?

I told myself that if I just worked harder, stopped procrastinating, had more hours in the day, was more efficient...then I would finally get what I'd been dreaming of. I'd finally make a big income and feel successful.

And yet, I didn't know what to do differently in order to be, do, and have *more*.

It seemed to everyone that I had a good life. But I was hiding a secret: **It wasn't enough for me.**

Whether I was making a lot, or a little, I constantly worried about money. I was stressed about how I could contribute more and make up the difference between my family's needs and my big dreams.

On the rare occasions when we went out to dinner, I would choose my menu items based on the price, not on what actually sounded good to eat.

Meanwhile, I was helping my clients create internationally-known online brands and generate leads that produced hundreds of thousands of dollars in sales!

I FINALLY LEARNED THAT NOTHING WOULD CHANGE UNLESS I DID

And I set about changing myself and my beliefs about money - and guess what? I did it! I've transformed my relationship with money - and it is a *relationship* - so I know it's possible for you, too.

How about you? What are your versions of these beliefs? Which feel especially true for you?

Here's where I'd like you to get started writing your new money story:

Put this book down for five minutes and use your workbook from lifewithpassion.com/bookbonus to really process this through.

List your five to ten top-of-mind money beliefs you've learned along the way (like the ones I listed above).

Then write down what you would choose to believe, instead (most likely, it's the opposite of what you've learned).

For example: "There's never enough"

Turn that into: "I always have enough money for all of my desires."

Do this for your five to ten initial beliefs, then read the NEW beliefs to yourself at least once a day, either first thing in the morning, or right before you go to bed, or both. Do this for twenty-one days at a minimum, even if it feels like you're lying to yourself at first. Over time, notice how you feel as you say the new beliefs.

Even better, I want you to take the positive beliefs you wrote down, and write them on sticky notes.

Plaster them everywhere - your mirror, the dashboard of your car, your kitchen.

Buy AquaNotes and slap up these new beliefs in the shower.

Set reminders on your phone, make them your computer and phone desktop, make a positive phrase your computer password (mine's my current monthly income goal!).

These notes will catch you as you're going about your day and snap you out of your old thought habits into new ones.

Because you're repeating these positive beliefs over and over, all day long, you're actually changing the patterns in your brain. Instead of the old pathways your thoughts used to travel – the ones that have kept you from have a great relationship with money – your thoughts begin to travel new pathways in your brain. You are, quite literally, changing your brain!

Just realize that you've been traveling those old pathways a very long time, so be patient with yourself if it seems to take a while to ingrain these new thoughts.

Did you do the steps above yet? If not, please stop and do them! Where are you going to put your paper and digital sticky notes, so you have to read them all day long?

"I CAN'T AFFORD IT."

Listen, I know money is a very sensitive and painful topic for many people.

And so often I see women holding themselves back because they say they don't have the money to pursue their dreams.

We've already talked about banishing the victimizing word "I can't" from your vocabulary, but I'm bringing it up again because this one is just so ubiquitous and *it seems so rational* that you might not think to eliminate it!

When you say you can't afford it, **what it actually means is you don't value this enough to pay for it** or to find a way to pay for it (and yes, I have said it myself!).

You may have heard that anger is a secondary emotion. That means that anger is an emotion resulting from an underlying primary emotion like pride, embarrassment or fear.

Well, similarly, **money is a secondary reason for not doing something.**

Some of you may be thinking, *"That's crazy! That makes no sense! If you saw my bank account, you'd agree!"* But I'm telling you that money is just a tool. Money simply represents what you value.

For instance, if someone had said to me, "If you raise a million dollars in the next 24 hours, Maeve will live," you bet I would have shown up with that money. I don't care if I had to borrow everything I could, call everyone I could think of, and even become homeless on the STREET, without any possessions of my own, I would have DONE it. I'm 100% confident I could have made a million dollars materialize out of thin air to save her life if I was given the chance.

Why? Because I value her life that much.

I realize that's an extreme example, but most people just aren't that fierce about showing up for their dreams and their lives. When presented with the choice, most people blame a lack of money as the reason for not going all out. My client, Mallory, almost did that too:

> I felt like I knew Christine was a person I needed to be with, but I allowed my finances to get in the way. I thought, "I can't afford it, I cannot do coaching with her." She did a live stream later that same day in which she said, "Do not allow your finances to restrict the life you want to live." It was

a kick in the butt, and I said, "I need to figure this out, because I'm not happy and I'm not living the life I want to live. I signed up with her, had amazing coaching and I was eventually able to put in my resignation at work."

Consider for a moment the resources you have available to you because you live in a "first world" country of wealth. No matter what your job situation is today, no matter what your life has been like, no matter what your life circumstances are... when you look around, **the truth is that you and I are richer than 99% of the world.** Just comparatively speaking, we are in the 1% of the world, and we have access to resources that the other 99% do not.

Knowing this, it's truly a *limiting belief* that's holding you back if you say you don't have the money to make an investment in yourself. It's a matter of priorities. **If you want something badly enough you'll find a way to do it, right?**

So, take a moment to consider, what is that thing that you really want, but believe you can't have because of a perceived lack of money?

Write that in your workbook and then ask yourself, is that really true? Is there really no way in the world that I could actually imagine a scenario in which I could have that? Or can I find even 1% of myself that believes that I could make it happen?

Chances are good that more than 1% of you already believes that, because it's something you desire, but you just haven't been giving yourself permission to pursue it.

I know you're a passionate person. You have big, audacious dreams. Maybe you're scared they're not possible or you don't know how to get there. **But man, you want them!** So it's time to turn off that constant refrain of "Oh well, I would if I had the money. Must be nice for them...." *while you watch someone else make their dreams happen.*

It's time to pay attention and say "If they're doing it, maybe that means I can figure out a way to do it. I'm strong. I'm smart. I'm independent." You need to **put your money where your mouth is** and take a stand for those dreams, knowing that until your behavior changes, nothing in your life is going to change.

In his insightful article, **"Want To Become A Multi-Millionaire? Do These 14 Things Immediately,"** Benjamin P. Hardy shares the very first thing you should do:

INVEST AT LEAST 10% OF YOUR INCOME IN YOURSELF

If you don't pay for something, you rarely pay attention.

Most people want stuff that's free. But if you get something for free, you rarely prize that thing. You rarely take it seriously.

How much do you invest in yourself?

How committed are you to yourself?

If you aren't investing in yourself, then you don't have any skin in the game of your own life.

When it comes to self-improvement, investing 10% of your income on yourself will yield a 100X or more return on that investment. For every dollar you spend on your education, skills, and relationships, you'll get at least 100 dollars back in return.

If you want to do something extremely well, you need to surround yourself with the right mentors. Anything that you'll ever do well will be the result of high quality mentoring. If you suck at something, it's because you haven't received quality mentoring in that thing.

The best mentorships are the ones where you pay your mentor. Often, the more you pay the better, because you'll take the relationship far more seriously. You won't solely be taking in that relationship. You won't purely be a consumer. Instead, you'll be invested, and as such, you'll listen more carefully. You'll care more. You'll be more thoughtful and engaged. There will be higher consequences for not succeeding...How much money and time do you spend on entertainment, clothes, or food? It's a matter of priority.

It's only when you invest in something that you have the motivation to make it happen.

Your level of success can generally be directly measured by your level of investment. If you're not getting the results you want, it's because you haven't invested enough to get those results.

Your number one investment must be yourself.

Or, as Benjamin Franklin said much more succinctly, "An investment in knowledge pays the best interest."

When you choose to invest in yourself first, then you become the KIND of person who's capable of running a successful business.

Then you get clear on the money you desire to make (we'll talk about the "hows" soon, I promise), and you become a person who can easily sell services without the things you THINK you need in order to sell... like a website. Like a fancy logo. Like a bunch of systems and structures.

My clients regularly sell their premium-priced packages without a website. They're clear on their value, the client they serve, and they make relationships that quickly build the "know, like and trust" factor with potential clients; yes, even online.

Congratulations on being open to becoming aware of and changing your money story. That's something most people spend their entire lives unconscious of, or blaming others for.

Now that you know how to change your thought patterns, the power is truly in your hands to rewrite your story and even to change your family tree with your new thoughts about money and how they serve you.

Be sure to use the prompts in the workbook at lifewithpassion.com/bookbonus to help you begin to upgrade your thoughts about money now!

CHAPTER 7
CONQUERING FEAR &
SELF-DOUBT

"Everything you've ever wanted is on the

other side of fear."

– GEORGE ADDAIR

I've noticed a common theme when working with over-achievers and perfectionists: They all deal with the evil twins, fear and self-doubt. I spend more time working with my clients on these mindset principles than on any business system or structure, because until you learn to manage them, you won't be sustainably successful in business.

If you dream big dreams like I do, you've almost certainly come up against a deep-seated doubt - and its twin, fear - in your ability to achieve your goals.

The two are toxic best friends.

What do you call your fear? "Practicality?" "Being realistic?" "Lack of money?" I'm here to tell you that you are actually dealing with FEAR and *you are letting it hold you back!*

FEAR IS THE NUMBER ONE BIGGEST DETERRENT, DETRACTOR, AND FACTOR IN HOLDING YOU BACK FROM THE LIFE OF YOUR DREAMS

I'll tell you how I know that: it's my confession. In the past, I allowed self-doubt to pretty much control me. Don't get me wrong; I had made the leap into running my own business, and I was successfully helping amazing clients around the country... but my dreams were even bigger.

I wanted to make a HUGE impact on thousands of lives around the WORLD.

Unfortunately, I had a lot of excuses for why I might not be able to do it. My self-doubt was in full swing! My subconscious mind focused on all the risks involved and kicked in big-time, trying to keep me "safe" (which meant staying stuck where I was).

What are your excuses? What's been holding you back so far? Why don't you feel ready?

What if I told you: **you are, in actual fact, ready?**

I'm sure your mind is going into overdrive, telling you all

the reasons I'm wrong: you aren't "ready".

But I'm not wrong. You are ready (tough love). Because every other person who started anything was once where you are, right now. And they started anyway.

Here are some of the self-doubting thoughts that took up residence in my brain; see if any of them sound familiar to you:

- I'm scared
- I might fail
- People will judge me or criticize me
- I don't know where to start or HOW
- Someone else has already done it and they are way smarter/prettier/better/richer/farther along than I am
- I'm not sure it's going to work
- I don't have the money
- I am already too busy
- I don't have time to do it right, so why bother?
- I'm already overwhelmed
- I'm good at what I do, so I should just settle here and be happy with it
- What if I don't make the money back?
- What if it turns out to be a mistake?
- What if people think I'm stupid?
- What if no one buys what I'm selling?

Just like I believed there was never enough money, I

constantly told myself I wasn't good enough, and I had a whole laundry list of reasons why. I compared myself to others and always found myself wanting. I knew there had to be a better way, and I envied those who seemed more confident than I was, but I couldn't seem to find it for myself.

All these thoughts were coming from the mind of a person who had already accomplished SO much... yet I couldn't seem to get past them - for YEARS! I finally did, and here's how you can too (much faster than I did)!

BE HONEST

Being honest about your doubt or fear, and admitting it, is the first step in facing it head-on. If you know what your biggest doubt is, you can deal with it. By normalizing self-doubt, you take away the shame around it, become aware that it's not a character flaw, but something that can be changed, and you can begin to feel worthy. If you pretend your fear isn't there, it just grows.

At any given moment, only about 5% of what's going on in your brain is related to conscious thought. The rest is related to either automatic body functions, or to unconscious thoughts, based on beliefs. That means that unconscious fear is much more powerful than dealing with fear on the surface. You can't move past your innate fears until you're ready to face them, and the first step in facing them is just being aware that you have them in the first place!

So let's name fear and take away its power! Just like

Meryl did:

> When I started working with Christine I came face
> to face with how negative my thinking was and
> how destructive my self-doubt was. I couldn't be-
> lieve that there was any way I would be a success-
> ful entrepreneur. I was sure I would be the one cli-
> ent failure Christine would have and I was com-
> pletely freaked out at how much money I had
> spent to work with a coach. I had never done an-
> ything like this and it was so frightening!

And Morgan, a recent college grad who, before working
with me, said,

> I had little direction or idea of what my life could
> be like, paired with a crippling fear of finding my-
> self miserable in a job I hate five, ten, fifteen years
> down the road. I had exited the phase of life where
> much was prescribed, ie. course loads, coming of
> age requirements, etc... and I was lost."

Once you face it, then taking ACTION, however small,
will tell your mind that you are making a different choice,
and **tell those anxious thoughts to back off.**

FOCUS ON YOUR "WHY"

It's not just about you, it's about your why and what you're on a mission to do... whom you desire to help.

Let's face it, even if you have a really powerful "why", it still won't be enough if you allow your self-doubt and fear to continue to control you. I certainly wouldn't be here, right now, if I had.

What would it MEAN to your ability to fulfill your dreams if you take action in spite of your self-doubt? What would actually building your business do FOR YOU? And for those you love?

Think about why building your business is important to you! Connect to what's possible, and also to the reality that it won't happen if you keep allowing self-doubt to control you. Take action in service of that bigger "why."

Through our work together, Alayna has realized, "I deserve to create the life for myself and my family that I want," and she comes back to that when she's doing something new or a little uncomfortable. It's totally worth it if you're creating the life you want to live for yourself and your family, right?

When I read my list of "whys", I get inspired to take action! Try it!

ASK A BETTER QUESTION

Here's a truth: The longer you ruminate on your fears and doubts, the longer you stay stuck right where you are.

For example, if you are constantly questioning IF this

business is going to work, or what's going to happen if it doesn't, or what if you fail, or what if, what if, what if...you're keeping yourself in a "cycle of perpetual sameness."

Meaning, if you've been asking yourself these types of negative questions for a long time - a week, a month, a year - you're just recreating that old story over and over.

How about instead of asking, "What if this business doesn't work?" ask yourself, "What if it *does*?" That shift opens up your brain to think positively about it and start looking for reasons it WILL, rather than reasons it won't.

DEAL WITH IMPOSTER SYNDROME

Have you ever thought, "I'm afraid someone's going to ask me a question I don't know the answer to!"?

Guess what? That kind of thinking has kept you from reaching out to potential customers, getting on calls, and even making offers to book clients.

The fear of being "found out" is called imposter syndrome, and it can hold you back from a lot of things. Even if - from the outside - you look like you have it all together. Like I did, or like Ashley did while she had a successful marketing job... we both struggled with imposter syndrome.

The truth is, no matter how much you actually know, you never have ALL the answers, and even when you think you do - you think you've prepared to the utmost - you can still get surprised. But that's not a BAD thing. Let me tell you why.

That's what happened to me during my interview with John Lee Dumas for his top-rated iTunes podcast, *Entrepreneur on Fire*. I'd been prepping for my interview for WEEKS, had the answers to his scripted questions in front of me, and was all set...but then my carefully tested tech wasn't working right, (and he's famously on-time and super-strictly-scheduled).

I'd prepared ahead of time with the flow of questions and he usually sticks very closely to that, but not this time.

We managed to get through the tech issue, but within two minutes of the start, JLD threw a curveball question at me that made me literally start sweating. He uncharacteristically went off script, and I froze. You can hear the moment at 1:40 here (along with the rest of the episode).

I'd just proudly shared my success rate of helping over 70% of my clients who came to me in a "9 to 5" quit their jobs, and then he immediately responded, "Let's talk about the 30%. Why do you think that three out of every ten are failing, even though you're essentially giving them that path to greatness?"

I froze. I blanked.

In my mind, I felt like I stuttered for 30 seconds and then inanely responded with something ridiculous, mumbling what felt like an excuse and metaphorically hanging my head in shame.

And the interview went on, but I was honestly so frazzled that after we wrapped up and were chatting, I asked him, "Was that OK?"

For two months between the date of the recording and the air date, I worried about it and beat myself up about it.

On the day the interview came out, I couldn't even make myself listen to it until that night. But when I got to the dreaded moment, cringing with anticipation... it really wasn't even noticeable.

The horror was literally all in my head.

I showed up, and it went much better than I had thought. And like so much of business-building, showing up is the key.

I'm encouraging you to decide if showing up is something that will help move your business forward, without letting fear be in control.

I could have asked him to take it down, or not air it, fearing it wasn't perfect. But I'm so glad I didn't, because it's led to more amazing opportunities for visibility, for connecting with a whole new audience of women around the world, AND it's led directly to paying clients who share my values and passion.

So even though I was uncomfortable, and worried, and fearful, was it worth it?

YES.

I wouldn't trade it for anything, and now I'm even more confident in the next opportunity; I know I can handle whatever comes!

Remember

An exercise I often do with my private clients is to have them write down everything they've accomplished in their life. I call it a Confidence Resume.

Spend some time on this over the course of a couple of days - your brain will work on it while you're sleeping.

But here's the kicker for a lot of people: I want you to write down the "bad" things too.

That's right, go there. Use the great stuff as well as the awful and challenging stuff to fuel your self-belief.

You've probably experienced - and survived - things that others can't imagine. To you, they may be or have been normal. Divorce, sickness, abuse, death, job loss or change, moving, financial trouble—getting up and going about your day with any of these or a host of other stressors is often a heroic task. Recognize and congratulate yourself for doing so, and use the knowledge that you survived these things to fuel your mission and ability to take action toward it.

I'm going to share a very personal example and I want you to hang with me on this. I don't say this to shock you, but to show you how you can use the bad in your life to fuel the good in your future.

Whenever I get overwhelmed by a problem that causes me to doubt myself or my decisions, or to be afraid of what people might think of me, all I have to do is think of my stillborn daughter's tiny box of ashes.

I remember the moment the funeral home director

handed me the box, a look of terror on her face as she nervously waited to see how I'd handle this grief that she obviously wasn't comfortable with. I remember that moment, and all the moments since, that I've lived with the reality that box represents, and I access a deep, powerful strength I didn't know I had before her loss.

This experience provides a massive dose of perspective, in the same way that reflecting on what you survived can give to you.

So create your Confidence Resume of the things you've accomplished in your life, as well as survived. Go as far back in your life as you can, and READ IT DAILY. Note awards, honors, scholarships, extracurriculars, things you're proud of, things others have recognized you for, compliments you've received.

Remember (and write down!) what you won in high school, your achievements on projects or in extracurricular clubs at university, your grades, the things you've accomplished at work, your relationships, you name it. Anything and everything that you've achieved. If you want my help with this, you can grab an exclusive template in my Know Your Niche self-study program

http://bit.ly/know-your-niche-challenge

You're pretty awesome, right?

If you have trouble coming up with this, ask people who are close to you what they see in you.

Usually overachievers and perfectionists feel that whatever they do, it's never enough, so they don't give themselves credit for what they have done. Putting it on paper helps create a sense of healthy pride and recognition that organically diminishes fear and self-doubt.

Most people don't walk around with the natural confidence that could come from having accomplished everything you have accomplished. **Look at this list and remind yourself. It's powerful.**

Just listen to what my clients have to say about this process:

> I was having a case of serious self-doubt. After laying out my confidence resume, with Christine's help, I realized that I really did have a tremendous amount of knowledge and experience to teach others. – Caitlin

> One of the first projects Christine proposed was a confidence resume and the process of completing that was a revelation! I had been so brave in my youth and somehow had lost that self-awareness over the years. – Meryl

START YOUR DAY PROACTIVELY

Start each morning writing whom you choose to be, what you choose to believe, and how you want to replace your fear with constructive thoughts. Remember, **you happen to your** day, not the other way around.

Too many people start their days reacting, dodging, and recovering from whatever comes at them. This stressful start to the day breeds fear and an underlying sense of being scattered that takes you far away from your best, most confident self.

Decide how you want to show up in the world today. Do you want to be more confident and less afraid? Then decide you will be confident. Focus on what you CHOOSE to be, instead of what you're afraid of or *don't* want to be. As T. Harv Eker says, "What you focus on expands," so make that positive rather than negative.

Set a timer on your phone for five minutes, lock yourself in the bathroom if you have to, and decide how you want your day to go. If at all possible, write it down by hand. Determine what's important to you today and commit to accomplishing it.

BREATHE DEEPLY

> *"You should sit in meditation for twenty minutes a day. Unless you're too busy, then you should sit for an hour."*
> – ZEN SAYING

If I had read this saying a few years ago, I would have

thought it was ridiculous. But when a doctor told me I was literally going to DIE if I didn't learn to stop pushing so hard and actually slow down, I started being just the slightest bit open to it.

I used to scoff at this suggestion. Seriously, for years I wrote it off, believing it was too simple to work. But now I understand the science behind it. Intentional deep breathing activates the relaxation response in your body and gives your poor, chronically stressed nervous system permission to take a breather. Not only that, but your body needs to be able to differentiate between an actual life-or-death scenario and an anxiety-producing to-do list. Slow deep breaths help you keep life in conscious perspective.

FIND LIKE-MINDED PEOPLE

Research shows that you learn, grow, and achieve your goals much faster when you have support from peers and mentors. So stop looking for help from people who don't think like you *want* to think. Ask yourself,

"Whom do I need to be to get what I want to get?"

...and find the people who are already doing those things or acting in those ways. Ask them for help. Successful people are often happy to help, because someone helped them at one point, and they want to pay it forward. As we discussed in the last chapter, the best kind of mentor is one you pay, because you both show up more fully for the work.

I waited way too long to start working out of a shared

space with other entrepreneurs. I sat in my home office by myself, feeling isolated from the real world, and it took a toll. Even as an introvert, my energy, creativity, motivation and inspiration are much higher when I surround myself with others on this journey, and yours will be, too.

Nancy Rich-Gutierrez counts it one of the top results she's gained from our work together:

> With Christine's help, I have been able to narrow down my exact Zone of Genius and focus my efforts on what I'm best at. My eyes have been opened to a new and exciting way of looking at life, work, income, and business. I have made a large amount of progress personally and professionally in my outlook and mindset, and I have connected with a ton of equally inspiring women through Christine's extensive network of entrepreneurs.

GET SUPPORT

The very first time I put up a post announcing my new business, I almost threw up. Literally. I had so much nervous energy that it had to come out in some way.

Have you ever been that nervous? Have you heard that frightened voice saying, "You know, you don't HAVE to do this. Not doing this would be sooooo much easier than doing it." If I hadn't had my coach there, encouraging me and holding me accountable, I would've taken a lot longer to pull the trigger on my own business... if at all.

The first person who applied to work with me caused me some minor terror. What if I can't help her? What if I say something wrong? What if she doesn't want to work with me? What if she DOES want to work with me? :-)

As I grow to each new milestone and level in my business, I still have to manage my fears, but it HAS gotten easier. Now, since I have gotten support to move past the fears, I recognize them for what they are, and they don't control me or stop me. I discovered that when I have trouble believing in myself, the quickest way to get where I want to be is to get support from someone who's been there.

In order to face my fears and discover how to actually *use* them to create the business of my dreams, I needed to find and work with someone who'd been where I was going... who'd walked the same path I was walking... and who could help me shorten the timeline to better results. So I didn't wait for my self-doubt to dissipate before I got support. I realized that getting support was the KEY to building a consistent business where I was no longer holding myself back.

When you're confused about all the things that contribute to a satisfying, successful business - whom you're serving; identifying your "Zone of Genius", as Gay Hendricks, PhD. calls it in his outstanding book, *The Big Leap*, and which strategy to use - getting support is the bridge between where you are and where you want to be.

As Ashley said,

> A few of the things I've struggled with are im-
> poster syndrome, lack of clarity on my purpose,
> confidence levels lower than the bottom of the sea,
> and both a hearty fear of failure and success.
> Christine's reassurance, reminders of my pur-
> pose, and her strategic action steps (only if they
> feel good and authentic!) are what drive me to
> continue reaching for my dreams. When you've
> been taught how to be an employee your entire
> life, it's extremely hard to believe that you can -
> and deserve to - live life on your own terms. Snag
> a call with Christine and she'll make you feel like
> you can do ANYTHING, and then she'll help you
> figure out your next best steps.

THAT's the power of getting the right support.

Self-doubt is not a character flaw, it's just a thing most people face on the journey to success. How you deal with it will determine your destination.

DECIDE

"WORRY is a state of mind based upon fear...Worry is a form of sustained fear caused by indecision, and therefore it is a state of mind which can be controlled. An unsettled mind is HELP-LESS. Indecision makes an unsettled mind...There is only one known antidote...it is the habit of prompt and firm DECISION...you do not worry over conditions, once you have reached a decision to follow a definite line of action."

-NAPOLEON HILL

You know that coach - the one who was there for me when I nervously first announced my new business to the world? Well, when I first invested in her coaching program, I was totally freaked out (I'd never spent money on myself or my business before), but I realized that **making the DECI-SION was tantamount to moving forward with my goals.** It was accompanied by the option to do a day-long intensive at The Ritz London when the program ended, and I DE-CIDED that I was going to make this happen for myself.

Less than five months later, I found myself attending that intensive in a room used by Churchill, de Gaulle and Eisenhower during WWII. I also stayed in and had high tea at The Ritz, barely recognizing my life! In less than half a year, my income had tripled, my husband and I bought our dream home, and when we left London, we then spent two weeks in Italy, which I'd been dreaming of since high school! IN LESS THAN FIVE MONTHS!

That's what's possible for you, too, when you finally override your fear and worry, go with your gut, and MAKE A DECISION.

What can you DECIDE today, large or small, in order to move out of crippling worry, fear, and indecision? Where do YOU want to be in three months, six months, a year? And what kind of support are you going to put in place to make sure it happens? (Hint: if you haven't already started working through the free bonuses you get with this book, I highly recommend you go over to lifewithpassion.com/bookbonus and do that.)

ACTION - START WITH 5 MINUTES

MOST people let the fear of failure and its partner-in-crime, the fear of what people will think, control their ENTIRE lives. But that's not you, right? So how, exactly, do you conquer this super-common fear?

It's simple, but not necessarily easy: by TRYING THINGS.

Today, right now, choose something small, that's been scaring you, set a timer and do it for five minutes. It could be something like:

- Reaching out to a potential customer

- Following up with a potential customer
- Making a post on your personal page
- Introducing (or re-introducing) yourself in your favorite FB group
- Going on Facebook Live
- Putting pen to paper to process through your biggest goal or fear right now
- Figuring out how you can pay for that business investment you've been wanting to make but you're too scared to let yourself have
- Making a connection with someone you admire
- Being honest with someone close to you about your entrepreneurial dreams
- Deciding on a price for your offer
- Posting your offer on your business page

Try that one thing for five minutes, and experience the rush that comes from completing it. Build trust in yourself such that you CAN accomplish things... and when the big stuff comes, you'll be sooooooo much more confident and ready to just do it. What will you do for five minutes today?

With a consistent, persistent commitment to become confident and courageous, it WILL happen, and your business will reflect your newfound strength.

And ask yourself this: What's the worst that could happen if I do go for it? Literally, the worst thing? Let yourself really explore that in your mind.

And then ask: What will happen if I DON'T pursue this dream?

Jack Canfield says in *The Secret*,

> Think of a car driving through the night. The headlights only go a hundred to two hundred feet forward, and you can make it all the way from California to New York driving through the dark, because all you have to see is the next two hundred feet. And that's how life tends to unfold before us. If you just trust that the next two hundred feet will unfold after that, and the next two hundred feet will unfold after that, your life will keep unfolding. And it will eventually get you to the destination of whatever it is you truly want, because you want it.

It's time to take a stand for those dreams and for your commitment to them today.

Take that first step in faith. Try it for five minutes. Then tomorrow, repeat.

CHAPTER 8
CONFIDENCE +
CONSISTENCY =
SUCCESS

Confidence plants the seeds of your dreams, con-

sistency brings the harvest.

– MARK AMERMAN

I didn't always feel confident or clear about my business or who I served. In fact, one of the reasons I LOVE helping clients get clarity and focus is because I know exactly how bad it feels to be scattered and unsure, throwing stuff against the wall, wondering what's going to work, wishing I had that elusive surety that other people around me seemed to feel and display.

It's soooo common for high-achievers to get stuck, wondering if what you have to offer is any good, if people will want it, or if *you* are good enough/qualified enough/able enough for people to take you seriously, and if you can actually help your clients get the results you're promising.

If you're nodding your head right now, saying "YES, SISTER!" please know that it doesn't HAVE to stay this way. You *can* train your brain to believe and think differently.

People say to me all the time, "I could never do what you do! Just get on video and talk, LIVE?!?! Hold a webinar?!?! Go on a podcast or on TV? No way!!!"

I used to say the same thing, and now I LOVE IT!!!

And so do many of my clients, because, as Andrea says,

> I certainly managed to step way out of my comfort zone since I started working with Christine, but her coaching style is such that you don't actually realize what you are doing until you actually do it.

I'm sneaky that way!

> While working with Christine I essentially 'came out of the closet' by announcing on my social media feeds that I was starting a coaching business. I also started sharing a little bit more about myself and my personal story of struggle, and I've

adopted an attitude of a public speaker by hosting weekly lives on my feeds.

You could say that these were difficult things to do, and had I been on my own I would have never done them because of my limiting beliefs around success, knowledge, and self.

As a side note, Andrea did this for her Spanish-speaking audience in her native country of Bolivia, as well as for her English-speaking friends around the world!

Just two years ago, I couldn't have done these things myself, either. I thought if I was going to do a live stream or a webinar, I had to be very calm and straightforward because that is what I thought would make people think I was professional. Then one day I came across a 7-figure coach who was acting goofy and crazy on her livestreams, and I adored it. She was so fun and GENUINE! And I thought—*that's* the real me. That's who I've always been. My best friends knew that I was a lot of fun, but for a while, they were the only ones I let see that side of me.

So what changed?

With that realization, I started by just experimenting with showing that side of me online.

The result? Women started saying things like, "I love your energy!" They also became high-paying, ideal clients left and right BECAUSE of the way I was showing up as my real, authentic, genuine, WEIRD, self! Plus, it energized me rather than drained me, built my confidence even more, and taught me a super-valuable lesson about allowing myself to learn and grow along the way.

You're allowed to learn along the way, too, and you will evolve. You're allowed to completely change up the way you've been approaching something, especially if you realize you've been on the wrong track. But it starts with looking at why you're holding yourself back and doing *whatever you need to do* to build that confidence in yourself, because it is a learnable skill.

How do you build confidence? By taking action. By doing something NEW.

In Alayna's words, "Working with Christine gave me the confidence to start creating my strategy on how to create my business."

Did you catch that? **Creating the confidence came FIRST, then the aligned action and strategy.** And that's exactly why there are so many chapters on mindset before we further break down the simple "to-do" strategies we outlined in Chapter 3.

I waaaaaay overcomplicated it for a long time so I want to tell it to you simply: **It all starts with showing up.** That's it. Just showing up. Showing up and being visible DAILY in your business.

Are you doing that right now? If not, that's the place to start.

If so, and you're still not feeling confident and clear, start asking yourself, "What do I need right now?" Instead of throwing a little bit of everything everywhere, are you doing the one or two things each day that could actually get you more clients? Are you clear on what those are? I talk about getting visible in other chapters, which, when combined with confidence and consistency, is the key to getting clients.

Simplify, simplify, simplify… Focus on the fundamentals, the basics, and you'll get clarity and confidence in your expertise as a result.

This is why my framework is **simple strategies + self-belief**. Both are required.

THE TRUTH ABOUT "OVERNIGHT SUCCESSES"

Consistency is the key to building a business. It's not a one-time   offer-that-turns-into-a-7-figure-business-thing   - EVER - and if someone says it is, they're LYING TO YOU. LY-ING.

Sure, maybe someone had a post or article blow up once. But I guarantee you it wasn't the first thing they did in business. They first had to do the work of figuring out what their ideal audience wanted to hear, where those people were hanging out, and what valuable offer to make that would be a total no-brainer to say "yes" to.

So there's ALWAYS more behind-the-scenes work than you can see. It's like the iceberg analogy—most of it is unseen.

Example: I've had two articles featured on The Huffington Post, on the Business homepage and Lifestyle homepage. Great visibility, right? BUT. I first pitched Huffington Post back in November 2015. I was so disappointed that I didn't get approved (no response, no nothing) that it took me nine months to pitch again. This time, aha, I was in, even getting a personal email approving me from Arianna Huffington! Then, six months later, after consistently posting articles, I had my first one featured. It never would have happened if the first time I put an article out there, I thought, "This is doomed to fail because it didn't get featured; I obviously stink and so does my business," and I walked away.

Support is often key to having this kind of stick-tuitiveness. Find someone who gets it and who you admire to encourage you and pick you up when you're feeling down, so you'll try again. Keep showing up, and you're on the right track to a business you're proud of.

Like my client, June, said, "Christine has helped me gain confidence, not only in myself, but in the work I provide for my clients."

That's what the right mentor does for you.

In the beginning of my businesses, I struggled with a major up-and-down pattern of a big month, followed by nothing the next, then another big month, then nothing the next, and maybe even the one after that. I had big goals and ambitions, but I wasn't hitting my targets. **I kept asking** myself and everyone around me, "What am I missing?!?!"

I beat myself up, stressed myself out (not to mention my sweet, very structured husband) from the inconsistent income, and with jealousy and a spirit of competition watched others around me being consistent, feeling like they were getting farther ahead, and taking business from me.

I was coming from a place of desperation, so everyone seemed to be doing better than I was, and I kept coming up with a bunch of ideas, spreading myself thin, throwing stuff against the wall here and there to see if any of it would stick.

Not so pretty, eh? But you know I'm always going to be real with you, and that's the truth.

What finally changed for me?

My mentor challenged me to **get consistent**. She told me that before I started anything new, I needed to prove that I could be consistent for 90 days. Challenge accepted! I got focused, set ONE CLEAR GOAL of what I was going to sell and how I was going to sell it, and went for it.

When you get consistent for 90 days, you not only build your confidence, but you also build your self-trust that you are the kind of person who keeps showing up and can, and WILL, be successful.

Plus, you stop wasting so much energy questioning everything and can set about actually taking focused, strategic action.

As a result of all these things, you'll start to see results, which will reinforce your ability to keep going!

ARE YOU 60% SURE...
OR WAITING TO FEEL 100%?

Katty Kay and Claire Shipman, the authors of *The Confidence Code: The Science & Art of Self-Assurance--What Women Should Know*, found that men apply for a job when they consider themselves only 60% qualified, but women need to feel 100% qualified to apply!

WHAT?!?!?! How can this be?

Take ten seconds and really think about that. Let's say you look at a job description, or, in this case, think about a business you're considering starting or growing, and you only hit six of the ten bullet points required to make it a success. Well, if you're male, chances are you're going to believe you're qualified, and you're going to go for it.

But if you're a woman, it's likely you won't.

Doesn't that kind of tick you off?

I know it does me. Is the world missing out on what YOU have to offer because you're waiting to be 100% qualified? I've said before that *action relieves anxiety*, and you learn by DOING much more than by researching forever.

No more waiting on the sidelines!

Life is just too short to NOT try. You've got the opportunity in front of you, and it's yours for the taking. Why should someone else get success, and not you?

This is not a criticism. Believe me, I've been there, and MY list of "60% confidence level" is a mile long. Here's a list of times when I did something anyway, even if I wasn't 100%

confident:

- Announcing on Facebook that I was starting my business.

- Moving across the country without knowing a soul or visiting the town first.

- Quitting my job without guaranteed freelance work lined up.

- Getting my first horse. Graley was 5 months old, and I didn't know the first thing about owning a horse, much less a baby!

- Learning how to cook a chicken (Seriously. I used to have a major, discussed-in-therapy phobia of raw meat. But alas my body needs animal protein to properly function, so there you go.)

- Traveling to Salt Lake City, London, and Sochi to spend a month at each, working to help broadcast the Olympic Games.

- Becoming a college professor at age 23 without any formal training in how to teach students, teaching some of the same people I'd been in undergrad classes with!

- Getting a job as a career counselor without formal

training

- Having a baby

- Co-founding a nonprofit with my husband

- Producing a music video and a PBS documentary that won national and international awards

- Puppy-raising (and gave up!) two Golden Retrievers, Lucy and Ben, for work as service dogs

- Writing this book

I know you've got a similar list, just like my clients and I do!

Sherry came to me having already been able to quit her high-paying job, but with her confidence knocked down because she'd tried a bunch of things and spent a bunch of money to build her essential oil business, and none of them were working. She told me:

> I was frustrated and feeling totally confused. Do I continue? Do I switch gears? Why isn't anything working for me? I couldn't understand how I could put so much effort and money into learning what I needed to learn and not see results.

Being on the other side of each of those fears is indescribably freeing, encouraging, and confidence-boosting. I would've missed out on all that if I didn't get help to make it happen.

Did you catch that? *Having enough confidence isn't what caused me, or Sherry, or anyone else, to take the big step forward. Just like I had done before her, Sherry got help to get her to the point where she could take the step, THEN the confidence came from having done it.*

So, what are you considering that you're "only" 60% sure about? Or, looking back, what things were you petrified to do, but you did them anyway?

WHEN IT FEELS HARD

I recently hiked in Colorado above the clouds, above where even trees can live. I marveled at the resiliency, the capability, the wonder that is the human body and spirit. That we can, in a day, without preparation, traverse terrain uninhabitable by trees that have spent so many generations adapting to it...

It reminded me that we are SO capable. Sometimes building your business can feel hard or stressful or overwhelming...remember, you are FAR more capable than you know, or might feel, right now. You can climb a mountain, literally, and you can climb one figuratively, one step at a time, as you build the business of your dreams.

What's one "feat" you've accomplished that you're proud

of, personally or professionally?

Add that to your Confidence Resume and come back to it!!!

More proven strategies for building your confidence:

- Like with your money beliefs, listen to your self-doubts, then tell yourself the opposite, and write it down. Either way, it's just a story you believe that determines your reality, so you might as well choose a happy one!

- Get fierce about the things and people you care about, about the life you want to live and what it's going to take to get there.

- Follow the high. Do whichever tasks really make you feel AMAZING, and find ways to do more of that! If you want to be a copywriter, write an awesome proposal for a dream client! If you desire to serve as a coach or consultant, offer free calls where you pitch at the end. This will naturally get you results, energize you, and remind you what you're good at.

- Confidence is like a muscle. Work on it every day, just like working out. Read your Confidence Resume daily.

- Don't rely solely on yourself to start telling yourself a

different story; start getting HELP!!! Read books that teach you how to think differently. Talk to and surround yourself with positive people. Find a mentor.

The main thing to remember is this: you can start increasing your confidence RIGHT NOW. It won't take forever, it is possible, and it is key to your success.

How good does it feel to know that you can immediately start feeling more confident?

Now pick one of these strategies and get to it! Then come on over to my Facebook group and tell me what you did.

https://www.facebook.com/groups/lifewithpassionsociety/

CHAPTER 9
THE "HOWS"

"Clarity comes from engagement, not thought."

— MARIE FORLEO

This chapter introduces the final steps, 3 to 7, in the *Income Replacement Formula.* More detail on each of the steps is found in the following chapters.

Step 3 is Niche. Here, you determine exactly whom you're serving and what their needs are.

Step 4 is Offer. Once you know who you serve, it's time to discover the biggest problems faced by people in your niche and create a container for solving them!

Step 5 is Marketing. Sharing your offer with your people can be fun, and you're going to get some of my best strategies for doing just that.

Step 6 is Visibility. Here's a blueprint for becoming more

visible to a wider audience, so that they can connect with you and know you're the right person to help them!

Step 7 is Sales. Many people feel "icky" when it comes to the sales part of running their own business. Here's how to do it more authentically and without pressure on either side.

Like confidence, clarity comes from taking action, NOT from thinking, planning, Googling, and wasting time on endless research.

It's true. Some people think they have to have clarity and confidence BEFORE they can act… but the truth is just the opposite most of the time. You gain clarity and confidence only after you stop standing in one place and start moving *toward something*.

The best place to begin growing clarity and confidence is in the message you share with your audience. And that message starts with *your story*.

YOUR MESSAGING

Your story is what helps you become known, liked, and trusted by your ideal clients (also known in various circles as your avatar, target market, or niche).

People told me that sharing my story was important, but I dismissed it because I thought I didn't have anything interesting or dramatic enough to say... that my story didn't matter... that it wasn't unique enough. So I didn't talk about it in my first business. Now I know this was a really big mistake.

When Maeve died, I knew in my head that I could share this powerful experience... But I felt scared that people would think I was exploiting her if I talked about her in relation to my business. I didn't want to share my struggles because I didn't know if I could handle the judgment I felt sure I would receive.

Just like before, I was keeping myself small by being scared to use my story.

My first mentor challenged me to share my story and taught me the lesson that there is **no competition**, because your story is the one thing that no one else has. It's also the very thing that will make people want to work with you or buy from you.

In taking this challenge, I realized Maeve was THE REASON I started Life With Passion, so it was actually inauthentic of me NOT to talk about her, and you know I'm all about authenticity and being genuine.

I also realized that I was actually aiming that judgment at myself for not being perfect, and it was holding me back from serving the world. Once I began to accept myself, forgive myself, and embrace my whole journey, I experienced a new level of freedom and joy.

So I started talking about her in Facebook posts. I started

talking about her in videos, and on my webinars, and in articles and on podcasts.

And I discovered that most people didn't judge me, and those who did, didn't matter. I got to make my daughter famous, which allowed me to proactively answer my fear that she'd be forgotten. People around the world know her name now, and think of her with love.

This is the dream of every parent who's lost a child.

I also continued talking about my horses, who were the original driver behind me wanting to get free from my "9 to 5" (so I wasn't going to work in the dark and coming home in the dark and never getting to see them).

What happened?

These were the two things I became known for, that became synonymous with my name and message; I even get tagged in Facebook groups for these two things. They make me memorable, and help me stand out in a sea of coaches. But they are not the ONLY things I'm known for.

Now I work with my clients to help them own *all* parts of their stories... the things they discount, have forgotten, and the things that maybe they're scared to share. Doing so helps them become more known, liked (even loved!) and trusted, and to build their business quickly, in a genuine way.

Yes, I've worked with many clients who have a connection to horses or pregnancy loss, and I love that. But not ALL of them do - it hasn't niched me down too far or shut me out.

It's made me memorable.

Your story is the ONE THING no one else can EVER duplicate. Without it, you're probably not especially memorable.

The good news is that this can change today, and that it makes it so easy to come up with messaging that's magnetic to your niche!!!

Have there been parts of your story you've been afraid to share because you didn't want to be judged as an attention-seeker? What are you afraid people will think, say, or do when they read or hear that?

Is it worth not sharing it vs. being able to help the people who could benefit from hearing it?

Here's the lesson: Embrace and share your story. That's what makes you memorable.

Don't ever be afraid to use what makes you different. **Embrace both your unique gifts AND your challenges.** You can even use the worst thing that ever happened to you - you survived it, after all! - to create the business and life of your dreams.

THE ONE ODD QUESTION TO ASK YOURSELF

If you're already in the midst of building your business, you're probably looking for more clients or customers, right?

Or maybe you're still at the very beginning of building your business, and you're nervously wondering if there are any paying customers out there for you.

There's one question that will help you attract the people whom you'll love to serve, and who will love to work with you.

It's the question that quickly connected me to my ideal clients and gave me clarity in my business. It helped those people to find me.

Here it is:

What makes you weird?

That's it! It may sound simple, easy to ignore, but let me explain.

Ask yourself:

- How am I unique?
- What make me feel like the odd person out?
- What quirks do I have that would make me stand out in a room?

These are the very same things that will make you memorable to great-fit, long-term clients, because these will be the things that let them know you "get" them on a personal level.

What do I mean by weird? Here's an example from my own life:

One thing that's really weird about me is that even though I love nice things (believing I was/am worthy of them has been a huge journey for me in itself), I'm willing to get down and dirty for one reason alone: my horses.

Camping? No way; I'm out, give me my own bed or a swanky hotel room. Getting dirty and sweaty (unless I'm working out and immediately going to shower)? Hate it.

But guess what? I do it for my horses, and I love it. I throw on my barn boots, slop around in the mud, and come home with dirt on my face and in my hair, yet it's one of my absolute favorite things because it involves horses.

Then I'm going to come home, clean up, put on makeup, curl my hair, go out, and feel just as at home having a four-course meal at my favorite wine bar as I did covered in horse dirt.

This dichotomy makes me different—it makes me weird!

For a long time, though, I hid who I was (not only this, but other things, too) because I thought I was too strange a mix of things:

- I'm an introvert who loves performing for and being with people (on my terms)…
- On the Myers-Briggs, my personality type is the rarest (INFJ, less than 1% of the population)…
- I have a secret love of teen dramas…
- I love dark chocolate but hate milk chocolate, chocolate ice cream and cake…
- I love a $60 bottle of wine but I'm not afraid to drink wine out of a box!

…And a million other quirks.

I used to think, "There's no one like me, I don't fit in anywhere."

Can you relate?

Once I started sharing the things that make me weird, though, I found that more clients came to me, and those clients shared my weirdness, too! In fact, some of my very first clients were horse owners, and though my client base now encompasses many other types of women as well, this "weirdness" helped me stand out early on in my business.

That's how Angie Wells, the owner of Equine Essential Wellness, decided I was the right fit to help her rejuvenate her business (and she ended up quitting her job as a result!):

> When I first found Christine I was really frustrated and burned out. I had built a website on my own for my business, but I was so busy, also working full time and had a family to take care of. I was starting to procrastinate. I would sit down for hours to write content and not make any progress. Leads started to dwindle and my business started to suffer. I knew that if I continued in this pattern, my dreams and my business wouldn't be there anymore.

I searched for someone to help me for a few months before I found Christine. Since it's my business, I really needed someone who understood horses. When I listened to her audio series something inside me told me that this was what I needed to do next. I didn't know how I'd afford it or how I'd fit it into my schedule but I knew it had to be done. It was "do it or let your dreams die" and I wasn't about to let that happen!

I still get a little emotional thinking about where I am now in comparison to where I was then. After working together, my creativity is back, my passion is back. I thought that maybe I just worked too much or was just too busy, but in our first few calls, I realized it was the fear and the self-doubt that was holding me back... and that shocked me!

The tools and strategies Christine gave me really helped me move forward. Everything I was learning about my business started to resonate and fill my entire life. I trust my intuition now and follow through on it. For my business and my dreams, working with Christine really made a really big difference.

How can you apply this tangibly for yourself and your

business?

First, identify some of your personal quirks like I shared above. Then make a list, like the one below, of more character traits you have - it's very likely your ideal clients/niche will have them too!!!

I keep this list in front of me to help me determine if someone is a good fit for me:

- Driven, motivated high-achiever, others call her a "go-getter"
- Often recognized for her accomplishments
- Very capable
- Has received awards, scholarships

BUT...

- Feels that what she's done is never enough
- Is called to big things and hasn't been able to figure out how to do it on the scale of her dreams yet and that's very frustrating to her
- Is held back by self-doubt, anxiety, perfectionism, fear of failure
- Feels pressure about all the things she "should" be doing
- Isn't sure about what her unique gifts are or if anyone would pay her for them
- Doesn't know if she's fulfilling her purpose and not

sure how to get there

This is my ideal client because I've worked through these things myself, and I know exactly what she needs to move ahead in business: a clear simple plan and the accountability to follow through on it.

I got to the point where I could make the list above with clarity because I started with answering the simple question: "What makes me weird?"

And now, years into my 6-figure business, it's evolved beyond the fact that I love getting dirty if horses are involved, to the unique ways I support and encourage my clients through their self-doubt, help them quit and stay out of their jobs, and build businesses with simplicity and clarity.

And those things quickly help the right clients *know* that I'm the person to help them.

So, what makes you weird? And what's on your list?

YOUR FIRST OFFERINGS

Do some informal market research among your ideal clients and find the common threads. What are they struggling with most? What are they asking for? How can you help them?

Then, create a package to take them from where they are now to having the result they desire.

For example, my 6-month mentorship helps women grow online businesses so they can quit and stay out of the "9 to 5" world. We meet every other week on the phone, email in between, and it's totally customized to each person's needs.

For this level of service and access, I get to charge a premium price, and they get maximum results because they get focused attention, private coaching, and a package designed around exactly where they are now.

Start by creating your premium-priced package, so when you become more visible to your market, you'll have an offer ready to go, and you'll know exactly how to talk about it!

BECOMING VISIBLE

I frequently speak to women who are confused or stressed about what it means to be "visible" online, if they want to grow their business. Because they aren't sure how to "put themselves out there", or how to do it in a way that feels good for them - so it's not overwhelming or scary - they hide.

Before we talk about HOW to be visible, it's important to establish *why* it's key to your online business success.

WHY DOES VISIBILITY EVEN MATTER ANYWAY?

1. Being Visible Makes You Memorable.

People have to be able to find you and remember you! Being visible is how people discover and get to know you. They begin to feel that you are *their* person; you are the one who can help them.

If you're looking around at everyone else being visible, scrolling through Facebook, Instagram, etc. but not putting yourself and your stuff out there, guess what? You're consuming everyone else's visibility, but not producing your own! Which means… tough love here…you're showing up for everyone else's business, but not your own.

OK, now that you fully appreciate how important this is, let me assure you, you're not too far behind.

2. Being Visible Builds the "Know, Like and Trust" Factor.

Yes, this seems a bit intangible, but it's the emotional connection that makes people want to buy from you or hire you.

With "know, like and trust" in play, your potential clients feel like they:

- **Know you** enough to be able to relate to you and feel like you "get" them, their needs, and their desires. They know you have some things in common.
- **Like you** enough to believe they would enjoy learning from or buying from you, maybe even that you'd be friends in real life.
- **Trust you** enough to know that you can help them. People won't buy until they trust what or whom they're buying.

Think about the people you follow, have purchased

from, or would like to purchase from. Can you see how you move through each of these stages until you trust someone enough to buy? But you can't jump to the end; you have to walk through all three stages.

3. Being Visible Establishes (and eequires) Consistency.

I think most people know that one post does not create a business. But many people also have a desperate hope that, "If I put one post out there with my big idea then I'll book out my services or program right away."

When that doesn't happen after the first or second time you announce yourself to (what feels like) the whole world, you may get discouraged. You may jump right to feeling like a failure… and then start hiding out.

THE TRUTH IS THAT PEOPLE REALLY *ARE* WATCHING. THEY'RE *ALWAYS* WATCHING

Not in a creepy way, but more like, "Hmmmm, she seems really excited about what she's saying. I'll keep my eye on her and see what she says or does next."

It may be totally unconscious on their part, but it happens. And then when you do keep showing up, they start to recognize your name, recognize what you talk about, your photos, your writing style, and then they might check you out.

As I mentioned before, **THERE ARE NO OVER-NIGHT SUCCESSES.**

Every single person who seems to be an overnight success has been working on things behind-the-scenes for a long time before anyone ever noticed. They may not share that in their posts though, often because they're selling something that sounds like it can make you an overnight success! Don't believe it!

Business-building takes work. I don't say this to discourage you. I say this to be real, and because I know you're not afraid of putting in the work.

So much of this work is about showing up consistently... about being consistently visible. If there's one secret to business-building it's this: **consistent visibility with a consistent message.**

I want you to start right now.

Ok, ok, so now you're convinced you need to be visible in order to grow your business. But how? Here are some options.

PERSONAL ONLINE OUTREACH

If possible, I recommend that you get visible with your offer first to your warm market.

Why?

The people who already know, like, and trust you are the people who are most likely to buy from you!

Any *new* visibility you do is to cold traffic, which does

take longer to turn into paying clients.

But if you're reaching out or getting in front of people who already know you, a lot of the legwork is already done for you!

THE COURAGE TO GET VISIBLE

Getting visible or "putting yourself out there" is the thing that often scares people the most. Just like it was for me, it's the thing that strikes fear into my clients' hearts.

In 2016, my first full year running my company, Life With Passion, I got *really* visible. Remember how I told you that the first time I put up a post announcing my new business, I almost threw up? I told my mentor, "I'm either going to throw up or work out." I did the latter.

I used my background and degrees in media communication, got support and examples from my mentors, and most importantly, **I did it before I felt ready.**

I did it when my audience was a fraction of the size it is now, when I'd only worked with a few clients, when they didn't have the results they do now. I had no idea how to do livestreams and I was a perfectionist about them because I used to be a producer and documentarian.

I was scared and nervous. I wondered what would happen when people saw me.

It felt crazy to put myself out there because, before starting Life With Passion, **I was extremely private,** and I prided myself on the fact that, ironically, I had *never* advertised in my online marketing business (I stayed booked through referrals).

On the opposite end of the spectrum, nearly all of my Life With Passion clients came because I made myself visible; 95% came to me as strangers.

What changed?

I decided that people needed to hear my message and I wanted to reach as many women as possible.

I knew there were so many women desperate to quit their jobs, who wanted more meaning in their lives, and who were dreaming of making a big difference… But I also knew they felt confused, overwhelmed, and stuck about how to do it. I knew my mission was to help them understand that no matter what they'd been through, it was possible not only to survive, but to thrive.

It wasn't just about me and my fear anymore. It was about the bigger mission and those women who needed to hear it from me.

Learning to get visible and put myself out there led to some major accomplishments in 2016 like:

- Having an $18k month in January!

- Making $10k in 72 hours, despite working while raising a 5-week-old baby

- Working one-on-one with clients in three different countries and in five different time zones

- Celebrating with them as all became more confident and took massive action, and 70% were even able to quit their jobs!

- Appearing on my first podcast in August, followed by dozens more at the time of this writing

- Starting my own YouTube channel

- Being personally selected by Arianna Huffington to appear in The Huffington Post

- Appearing on The Today Show's blog

- Launching a non-profit, Miles with Maeve, raising over multiple five figures and counting, and being a featured speaker on its behalf at a charity gala

I share these things to demonstrate what's possible for you, too, when you overcome your fear. It *can* become easy, comfortable, and even *fun.*

You can do any of these things you want this year. None of it is *hard,* it just requires you to do whatever it takes to: get over your fear (you may need support for this, like I did); show up; and be strategic.

Listen to how fast things shifted for my client, Dr. Shannyn Pearce, DC, multi-6-figure chiropractor and women's health expert, who's bringing her practice online to help women start feeling better so they can truly love their life:

Christine is all about getting us more visible. So although I have always done things kind of like that, she gave me a lot of input about how to do videos! I definitely didn't know enough about where to put them and how to target them. She has really great advice, but most importantly, she makes it really applicable so I feel like, "Okay, I can do this! I can put this piece in place right now and start to see things change in a short amount of time."

By getting me excited again and teaching me those few things and helping me put those videos where they need to be, in one week I booked six new clients! That's huge, because our average patient will come in and spend somewhere between $3000 and $5000 in our office.

My schedule is filling up for these calls and this is just the beginning. We haven't even started getting a broader audience. This is just because I listened to her advice, we got things going, we did it quickly, we got things up and moving and the results have already started to pour in. So, I am really excited!

Now, ask yourself: What would increased visibility like

that do for *your* business? Or where do you most want to be visible right now? (It's ok if it's also the thing that scares you the most).

Now go get the support and accountability to make it happen, and serve the people who need you!

GETTING FREE PUBLICITY

There's a lot of hype out there that certain strategies are the *only* way to grow your business. But what if you're just starting up, or you're in a stage where you don't have the cash or the knowledge to run a bunch of paid ads, or to hire a publicist?

When I started my business, I was taught that the way to get clients and grow my business fast was through running Facebook ads, *lots of Facebook ads*. I was taught to run Facebook ads to an opt-in, to put those leads into a funnel, and the rest would take care of itself. (If you don't know what any of that means, it's fine. You don't need to yet.) I got the impression that clients would come pounding at my door, booking calls left and right, signing up to work with me.

Being new to the industry and knowing the power of Facebook ads, because I'd run them for clients for years in my previous marketing business, I believed the hype. I wound up spending nearly all of my profits to get clients, and it became a discouraging cycle; I did get conversions, but they cost a *lot*.

I wanted something better for myself and for my clients,

so I decided to try a different way, and what I've discovered has been revolutionary for my business.

These are the things I've done to grow my business *fast*, without using ads:

1. Identify podcasts and websites where your ideal clients are hanging out.

2. Create a compelling, personalized pitch that highlights the value you bring to the editor or podcaster and their audience.

3. When you appear on the show or site, offer a valuable freebie that's aligned to the topic you're discussing and the audience you're sharing it with.

How has this worked for me?

After initially growing my business exclusively using ads, I didn't spent a dime on them in 2017, and I totally booked out my private coaching practice.

I shifted my focus to the power of *free* visibility to get seen and known and sign up my ideal clients, and you can too. By appearing on podcasts I've experienced huge, organic growth in my business, including the opportunities to:

- Get my articles shared by influencers like Arianna Huffington

- Land over 20 podcasts where my ideal clients hang

out, including Entrepreneur on Fire, a "Best of iTunes" podcast!

- Increase my email list and Facebook group by 40% from these efforts alone

- Become a regular contributor AND score homepage features on The Huffington Post and on Thrive Global

- Work with more clients than ever before

So this stuff *works,* and if you're feeling frustrated that you can't grow and scale your business because you don't have the capital to do the "big strategy" that someone said you need, consider this your powerful alternative.

It gives your audience the chance to know, like and trust you on a much deeper level than if they just click on your ad and sign up for your free offer off the bat. Give it a try, and watch your business grow.

Now, as you get visible, you're going to be attracting your ideal client, and they're going to want to talk to you! So it's important that you **focus on learning how to do sales.**

But not in the way you might think...

Bottom-line: no matter how flashy your website, photos, or logo are, it ALL comes back to **connecting with people and making sales** (i.e. making money, making a profit, so you can stay in business for the long term).

I used to feel really confused and overwhelmed about this whole idea of **giving value, being of service, and building relationships in groups** and elsewhere in order to sell, because I wanted clients NOW and I thought those messages meant it had to take FOREVER.

But it doesn't.

Here's what works:

I discovered that **genuinely connecting with people** and ALSO learning how to ask for sales, consistently, in a way that actually felt GOOD to me was a total game-changer for my business and my bottom line (I didn't want to feel salesy, icky, slimy, or like I was pressuring them).

WHAT DOES GENUINELY CONNECTING LOOK LIKE FOR ME ON A DAILY AND WEEKLY BASIS?

DAILY:

- I post content for my niche (who I'm super-clear about. You must nail this FIRST!) in my Facebook group and one other group I love, and I respond to others' posts and comments in both places

- I respond to emails and FB messages about connecting

WEEKLY:

- I send a minimum of one email a week to my list, sharing a lesson I've learned

- I follow up with women I've talked to who I KNOW I can help

- I reach out and make new, personal connections with colleagues (i.e. not being "too good" to talk to someone who might not be ready to buy from me right now)

- I cast a broad net by pitching at least one podcast appearance and/or publishing an article

- I invite women to book calls with me (don't forget to do this!)

So how about you? Which of these visibility strategies feels good to you? Which are you excited to implement?

Remember, if you're not visible, you don't have a business, because no one knows about you or your awesome services! You can start small, of course, but do start. Spend just five minutes a day at the beginning. One email or post or outreach of some kind. Or crack open that workbook from lifewithpassion.com/bookbonus and actually use it.

You'll get that ball rolling and you'll feel amazing that you're actually doing it!

CHAPTER 10
MAKE AN OFFER THEY CAN'T REFUSE

"You don't have to be great to start, but you have

to start to be great."

– ZIG ZIGLAR

So, with all of these strategies we're discussing, how exactly do you tie it all together to replace your income? Everyone's situation is different, of course, but replacing your income with a service-based business generally looks like this:

1. START ON THE SIDE
I don't want you to quit your job cold-turkey and then figure

it all out after that. I believe in starting smart and strategically.

I built my first business on the side of my draining "9 to 5", and when I finally quit, I replaced my full-time income in the first month!

Even if you feel like you don't have time or clarity, you *can* start somewhere, right now.

You've heard me say it before, but it bears repeating that clarity and confidence both come from taking action first, *not* from trying to get clear or confident first. So if you want to quit your job, it's time to get serious about starting or growing your business on the side of your "9 to 5".

The great news is, this doesn't have to be overwhelming or require a total calendar overhaul.

Again, try just 5 minutes of action today, and see what that gets you. It can be any type of action. Sending an email. Making a call. Looking up something you need to know before taking your next step....Go ahead. I'll wait for you to do it and come back...

Did you do it?

How does that make you feel? Are you willing to do it again to get that freedom?

Take that information and carry it into your strategy for tomorrow.

2. FOCUS ONLY ON MONEY-MAKING TASKS

Identify and *write down* ONLY those things that move you forward - that make you money - so you can work on THOSE every day.

Start by identifying either how you *think* you'll be able to get clients (if you're new to being an entrepreneur), or how you *know* you've gotten clients in the past.

What I want to help you avoid is the feeling of confusion, being overwhelmed, and the resulting inaction that comes from following too many "experts". If you've heard you "have to" do X from one expert, and you "have to" do Y from another expert, and a third expert told you "you can't be successful" until you do Z, you'll feel so scattered and unfocused, you'll likely just end up scrolling through Facebook!

You might even find yourself like Caitlin, who identified as "the type of person to flit from idea to idea if I didn't immediately get the results I wanted, instead of taking the time to make changes to improve what was already working."

Or like Joanne Muturi, who shares,

> I was already eight or nine months into starting my business, and I was not doing as well as I wanted, because I did not have structure. I wanted to try everything under the sun to make it work, but when I met Christine, she taught me structure.

One of the best lessons I have had from her is having me to concentrate on my Zone Of Genius. She was very clear to me some of the areas where I am doing well. And she said to me, 'Joanne, those are your strengths...stick to those! If that works, stick to it.' And that is exactly what I did.

I would get what we call 'discovery calls' from my Facebook LIVEs, so I would do my best to convert those people into paying clients. And then the first one signed up and I got so much confidence to do it again. As a result, I was able to do it again, and again, and again.

There's a lot of busy work that *feels* necessary but is not directly making you money.

Keep yourself focused on your actual money-making tasks, and let those be enough while you're building your business on the side. Otherwise you'll waste a lot of your precious time "working on your business" but not moving forward in your number one goal of replacing your income.

Once again, let go of FOMO (Fear Of Missing Out), feeling like you need to be everywhere and do everything, and focus instead on money-making tasks.

If you don't know what your money-making tasks are, start by identifying them.

For example, have you connected with potential paying

clients....

- In a Facebook group?
- From a personal post you shared?
- Through a referral?
- Via your newsletter?
- Through an interview or article you wrote?

Reflect on what has brought you customers or warm leads in the past, and focus on doing *that* again today!

This strategy will serve you well even when you're out of your "9 to 5", because even when your time is freed up, the more focused you are, the faster you can grow your business.

And, if you don't yet know what those tasks are, **make it a priority to figure them out ASAP,** so that you can use your limited time wisely and efficiently.

3. CREATE AND SELL PREMIUM-PRICED SERVICES

Properly value your offers and price accordingly, not based on what everyone else around you is doing or what you think people in your area will pay.

Create a premium-priced, value-packed offer based on what you're good at, how you like to work and where you shine (your "Zone of Genius").

For instance, if you're looking to replace a $100,000 income, then you need to create a $5,000 package out of your expertise, and sell twenty of those in a year... just twenty; fewer than two a month. Do you think you can do that?

Yes, I know businesses have expenses, but if you take advantage of the tax deductions that support small business growth, and you cut back in areas that you needed to spend more on while in your "9 to 5" (usually things like gas, professional clothes, eating out), you may find it gets really close!

Hustling a lot of tiny, one-off services is going to take a lot more time and energy than a couple of premium-priced goods or services.

In many ways, it comes down to a numbers game, and if your audience is small, wouldn't you rather be selling a few higher-priced packages than many, many low-priced info-products?

You'll also learn how to sell in a way that feels good, and that will serve you more than any other skill as you build your business.

Before going on, go back and re-read those three steps (this is a short chapter; go look at it again!).

Just like you did with money back in Chapter 6, notice any resistance, limiting beliefs, and stories about "why not" that popped up in your head.

Here's an example: You might have a belief that no one will pay you a premium price to work with you and that it would be easier to sell a bunch of low-cost offers instead (this one's really common). You can reframe this to say instead, "I believe that the right people will buy my premium-priced packages because I know that I'm providing them with so much one-on-one attention and value, and that will help them their result so much faster."

See what I mean?

So use your workbook from

lifewithpassion.com/bookbonus

to write your limiting beliefs down, then set about reframing them to more positive ones, one by one!

CHAPTER 11
PLANNING YOUR LEAP

"If you really want to do something, you'll find a
way. If you don't, you'll find an excuse."
— JIM ROHN

You've heard a LOT about how to generate the simple strategies and self-belief you need in order to build a business and quit your job.

How do you know when the time is right for you?

Is it only when you've exceeded the income from your job, built up a cushion of at least a year's worth of savings, and found a steal of a deal on insurance?

Not necessarily.

The tipping point - the point at which you decide to hand in that resignation letter - is different for everyone.

Here was mine:

After four pretty depressing, toxic, lawsuit-worthy years at a job I couldn't see my way out of, I discovered an escape route... one that, for a long time, I was ashamed to admit. I got married.

But it wasn't my husband's income that allowed me to quit. The fact is, we each owned a house (in 2010; hello, housing crisis) and mine hadn't sold, despite repeated attempts. So on top of our student loans and consumer debts, we also had two mortgages.

The issue was that I was moving an hour and a half away from my job, which was just too far to commute. Given how little I was making, and how much time I would need to sit in the car every day, it made no sense to continue working for my employer.

It was actually the "out" I'd been praying for: I was looking for something external that would rescue me from my job, so I jumped on the opportunity to quit. For years, I was sorry to admit that I wasn't brave enough to do it on my own but in retrospect, I'm just grateful that God used this situation to get me out, because it had become clear that I was too afraid to do it on my own. I was terrified to leave, but I chose love over that fear. And it also happened to get me out of a job I hated.

Here's the reality of life the day I quit my job and started my new business

- I was $40k in debt

- I moved to a new city where I knew no one

- I was a MAJOR introvert, even more so from the stress of moving and being in a new marriage

- I had no recurring income

- I had no savings

- We had two houses

- I owned three horses, one on the way

- We had two dogs

- I was also dealing with anxiety and depression from YEARS of unfulfilling work, leaving me full of self-doubt

I share this mess of a situation because I want you to know that no matter what your situation, it's NOT hopeless!!! Even though I knew so little, and I was scared, anxious and overwhelmed, if I could do it, you absolutely can!

So... remember that whole debt thing I mentioned? This HAD to work.

I felt the pressure of my debt like it was crushing me. Feeling like I didn't have enough money - which, remember, I had *always* believed to be true - triggered me into PANIC mode; I'd go straight into a palpitating heart, short, ragged breaths… typical fight-or-flight feelings.

I had no idea how to manage those feelings. I thought I was above all that "gratitude list" stuff, and meditation because I was such a go-getter. (Pretty messed up logic, right?) I also didn't know about tapping/EFT then, which became a huge help later on.

Despite all that, the first month full-time in my own business, I fully replaced the income I would have earned from my job! People started hiring me for stuff left and right! It's like they were just waiting for permission, waiting to know I had time and space for them.

The checks started coming and I could barely believe it! I was actually doing it!

Yes, I was sitting at a bar in our outdated bachelor pad kitchen, using my husband's old PC laptop (it was sooooo slow…) because I was determined to buy my own Mac once the business could afford it… but I was doing it!!!

Kalila Bodden, MD and Freedom Lifestyle Coach, found her own version of this magical feeling through our work together, after leaving lucrative 6-figure careers in medicine and corporate:

> With my online coaching business, I am now able
> to travel with my husband on trips around the
> globe, as well as visit family in different countries
> (it's like getting paid to go on vacation!). Nothing

makes me happier than being able to coach clients from the comfort of my own home *[which, by the way, is on Grand Cayman! Kalila lives on Grand Cayman!]* or while visiting exotic destinations. Because coaching doesn't feel like 'work', I am in love with what I do and am always excited to turn on the laptop each morning to see who has booked calls and coaching sessions with me that day.

SO KNOWING THAT EVERYONE'S TIPPING POINT IS DIFFERENT, HOW DO YOU DECIDE?

You might be single, married, with or without kids, with or without access to insurance through a family member.

You might be feeling - with your strategies, your consistency, and your clarity - that you have time to keep building your business on the side... and you do want to keep it that way for a while.

Or you might find that you don't have time or bandwidth to do both AND be present for your family, so you might be willing to make some different choices in order to bridge the gap.

It may be time to delegate some of the tasks you hate while you're still in your job to leverage your precious little free time more effectively.

Like Jenna, who was making five figures in her side business while working a demanding job in television production. She was exhausting herself staying up until 3 am making daily graphics that anyone could do. As soon as she decided to delegate those graphics to someone for a small hourly rate, she began getting more sleep, having more energy to dedicate to her business, and to enjoy her life more!

In my case, because I had the chance to get totally focused, I replaced my income in the very first month.

KNOW YOUR NUMBER; WHAT ARE YOU AIMING FOR?

Let's write it out! It's much scarier when you DON'T know what it is! Take home pay, taxes, health insurance, all that! When it's written out, it becomes a lot more real - and a real number is something you can hit!

You can also feel a lot more empowered about what to charge in your packages by figuring out the hourly rate you're already making in your day job. Here's how to do that:

Take your annual income, ($50,000 as an example), divide it in half ($25,000) and take the first two numbers ($25). That's your rough hourly rate, if you work full-time.

This is a great starting point because if you're like many women, you might already feel comfortable charging what you're currently getting paid. Keep in mind, however, that when you quit your job, you can expect to bill AT MOST 20 hours per week, if you're super-efficient, so as soon as you're comfortable and confident, you're going to want to double that rate.

But, as you're just getting started, and as I've discussed before, it's most important to start with where you're comfortable while building up your belief, your testimonials, and your business.

MONITOR YOUR LEVELS OF CONFIDENCE, FEAR AND SELF-DOUBT

As you get closer and closer to making the leap, you might find that you begin to lose confidence.

That's totally normal, and it's ok! This is the time to double-down on your confidence work from Chapter 8.

MAKE SURE YOUR SUPPORT AND YOUR TRIBE ARE IN PLACE

Who's going to be walking this journey with you?

Who will you turn to for strategy and next steps, as well as to encourage you when you're having a rough day?

It's been my pleasure to do this for clients like Dr. Shannyn Pearce, DC:

> You may be like me and are already busy, and sometimes you feel like you are too busy to really go to that next level, or you are frustrated, or been burnt out, or a couple of things you did might have failed or backfired or blew up in your face, and you can lose a little bit of that confidence. "If

I try it again, what if it doesn't go as well? What if I lose money?" Those things can hold us back and it gets really easy to be comfortable and just decide that life is okay how it is. But okay is not great, and if you are somebody who really wants to see those big things happen in your lifetime, that is what Christine brings to every female entrepreneur: the ability to go and dominate the world in whatever category that you were called to do!

And she is the best person to just link arms with to get you to that next level, and celebrate when you have the wins and listen to you when you have the losses. But giving you the plans and the steps and light that fire under you to really go and do the thing!

I love Christine and I really truly feel like any female who either wants to leave their job, is already an entrepreneur, wants to go to the next level, or really just needs that encouragement, should work with Christine. Hands down she is the best one to do it!

Make sure you line these up first, before you do something you've never done before:

- Join a supportive group of women online, like my free, private Facebook community.

- Get an accountability buddy who's going through the same thing and can give you one-on-one support.

- Hire a coach who's been there, has helped their clients get the results you're looking for, and can walk alongside you every step of the way. This is the fastest way to speed up your timeline and your results.

Nicole Dlugosz, a corporate accountant who wanted to spend all day riding and teaching dressage rather than crunching numbers for big companies, says:

> I found Christine through a Facebook ad, and honestly I was a little skeptical. You know, so many people are marketing themselves as life coaches or career coaches, but Christine had horses in her ad and I was drawn to that. I thought, "Wow, someone who understands my passion!" So I went to her page, then into her Facebook group, and I really felt that when you can connect with someone and relate to them, that's when you can make the coaching process work.

Since then it's been really amazing. I surprised myself with what I've done in just a short amount of time working with Christine. I didn't think I'd actually quit my job, but I have. It's so freeing and amazing. I'm in the baby start-up phase, but I'm a lot farther than I thought I would be.

Honestly the biggest surprise to me was how much work I needed to do on a mindset shift, and building my confidence on what I'm trying to do here, what I'm trying to offer. I'm really surprised that I got to the point of being able to say, "I can do this, I am capable." The fear of failure, the fear of success - of not being able to really meet the expectations of people that I work with - had held me back a ton. I don't think I'd ever have quit my job; I'd still be miserable. I've never left a job and not had another job lined up, but I really feel in my heart that this was the right choice.

I'm well on my way and I'm so excited - the possibilities are there, and I'm finally believing it is possible to live my dreams. It's all because of the support I've gotten from Christine. Getting over that hump with someone who understands what you're going through, and really making you believe that you can do it, is key.

HAVE A PLAN

You don't need a five-year plan, but I do recommend you have a 90-day plan. Then you take the information you get from those first 90 days, and turn it into your next 90-day plan. Performance expert Todd Herman shares that our brains can't fully wrap around year-long goals. Those are visions instead. That's why New Year's resolutions don't work and rarely last past the end of January.

But your brain can wrap itself around 90-day goals and execute on them; focus on one quarter at a time.

Within those 90-day goals, break them down into 10-day sprint goals, and then further into daily goals.

When you're getting started with a plan, set yourself up for fast success by identifying just one main thing you'd like to get done on a given day, and make it doable (for example, do NOT try to set up a whole website if you've never done that before). Maybe it's reach out to five people. Maybe it's write and post something on social media.

Whatever it is, we've got to set you up for success, and that starts with simplifying everything down to bite-sized pieces.

CELEBRATE

It's so important to celebrate the progress you've made before, during and after you take the leap!

I think people are often afraid that if you celebrate something, you'll lose motivation to keep the momentum going…

like you'll stop caring.

The truth is, as you learn to celebrate the little wins and trust yourself, you'll discover greater internal motivation to keep going in a way that feels GOOD, instead of pressured. Instead of feeling like it's never enough, you'll make more progress when you reward yourself.

Why are these celebrations so important?

It's simple and I've said it before: WHAT YOU FOCUS ON EXPANDS.

So, for example, if you focus on the progress you're making in your business, marking your accomplishments with celebrations, it gets easier to make more progress. Like amazing Ashley has found:

> You don't even need to know what the hell you want to do other than you know you're ready to leave your lackluster "9 to 5" and that you have dreams of living a life of passion....

> You can expect the most amazing and authentic enthusiasm every single time you hop on the phone with her as well as answers to any and all questions you might have. She's helped me side-step issues, she's been the voice I needed while I was going through the darkest and hardest year of my life, she's helped me work through my deep

fears and she's cheered me on when I landed the first of many fantastic clients."

You, too, can find your personal cheerleader; just as I've been able to help Ashley do, so you also can remember to focus on all the little wins… and celebrate them.

Let me tell you why this is so important: the reticular activating system in your brain filters OUT what you *don't* pay attention to, and filters IN what you *do* pay attention to. Then it says, "Oh, this is important to her, let's notice more of that," and goes out to get you *more of the same*. It's not "woo woo;" it's brain science.

So, what do you want your brain to find? If it's more good things, that will inspire you to take more good, business-building action, then celebrate your progress EVERY DAY!!!

For me, celebrating can look as small as throwing a shot of raw honey in my daily organic jasmine green tea (which I usually drink straight), or it can be as fancy as planning a big trip, with lots of other examples in between. You just need to say, "I'm celebrating this!" and feel great about it!

So find ways to recognize this amazing work you're doing and let your brain know that you are creating your dreams!

Take these steps, trust yourself, get support in place, and you'll know when the time is right to leap!

CHAPTER 12
DON'T LIMIT YOUR SUCCESS

"Define success on your own terms, achieve it by
your own rules, and build a life
you're proud to live."
— ANNE SWEENEY

As you're moving down the road to quitting your 9-5, or when you're already out and working to stay out for good, it's important to be aware of the mindset and productivity challenges you'll likely encounter, so you can catch yourself before you fall into those traps!

STRUCTURING YOUR NEW SCHEDULE FOR SUCCESS

Let's jump ahead and say you've been building your business for a while now. You're discovering that you have more time in your schedule than you did when you were working both in your "9 to 5" and on your side business at the same time.

If your business is based at home, it's very easy to fall into the trap of not working on your business during your best working hours. Instead, you catch yourself doing household chores, preparing meals, or working on projects you've been wanting to do forever, but never had time for.

To help you manage these tempting distractions, I recommend that you set aside a regular place where all you do is work.

Start using a calendar not only to schedule meetings with other people, but for business-building tasks like creating content, getting visible, and following up with leads.

Now that you have time for more things, it's as important as ever to avoid "shiny object syndrome" and to double-down on the activities that have, in the past, helped you get clients and build your business. If you want to try additional business-building strategies, that's great. But first make sure you have consistent income and you're clear on what works before you experiment with other strategies, no matter how much some influencer insists they are "sure-fire" successes.

CLEAR THE FEAR OF SUCCESS

Many women tell me they have a "fear of failure", but did you also know it's possible to have a "fear of success"? If you say any of the following to yourself, you're holding yourself back!

- I'm afraid that if I grow my business I'll be too busy and won't have time for my friends or family.

- I'm afraid I won't be able to do it all or I won't be able to manage if my business really takes off.

- I'm afraid if I put it out there I may not attract the right people... but what if I DO? Then what?

- I'm afraid I won't have enough time to devote to my full-time job.

- I'm afraid I won't be able to help clients when they come to me.

- I'm afraid I'll have some confrontation or conflict.

- I'm afraid I'll lose relationships from the people who don't really understand what it's like to run your own business.

Can you relate to any of these? These are all sneaky ways you might be sabotaging your success.

Remember, fear is always about keeping you SAFE. The

part of your brain that creates fear is really good at coming up with ways to make even a good thing - something like success - sound scary and not worth doing.

Even if safe means working a crappy job that you hate.

Even if safe means being miserable.

Even if safe means being and feeling STUCK.

Remember that to your brain, "safe" = "same". In other words, don't rock the boat, and I'll be safe!

If you have a fear of success, I want to help you move through that. The fear of success is very real and it's something I've experienced, too.

I have caught myself along my journey, thinking, "I'm afraid if my business gets bigger, I'm going to be too busy. Too busy to be present with my family, with my horses, with the people and things I love." I have even let the fear of success keep me stuck when trying to write this very book!

So has my client, Dr. Shannyn Pearce, DC, who was already a highly successful entrepreneur when we started working together:

> You do the same things for so long and you do them over and over again, it gets really tempting just to say, "You know we have done a lot and we can settle here. Or, maybe I don't have to go to that next level. Maybe life is comfortable right where we are.

When I talk to Christine, she really puts a lot of that into perspective. I feel like I leave every conversation just energized and ready to do it again. Ready to take on the world again and do whatever is next and be happy and joyful doing it, which is so important! Especially for female entrepreneurs. There are just so many distractions and things that can happen, that having a sounding board and coach like her to really get you back in the game, is the difference between winning and losing. It really comes down to that.

So, that is huge for me. That is, by far, my biggest frustration, just finding the encouragement and the help to keep going on what I know that I want to do. So I love when we come out of those conversations and I feel on fire again.

If you struggle with this fear, you are not alone. I'll happily raise my hand and say, "Me too!"

I didn't let it *keep* me stuck though. I managed to work through that fear and quickly build a six-figure business, simply by recognizing it, dealing with it, and moving forward anyway.

HERE ARE 3 TIPS TO HELP YOU MOVE THROUGH THE FEAR OF SUCCESS:

1. Acknowledge What's Going On

First of all, I noticed and acknowledged the fear of success that was holding me back.

Instead of beating myself up about it any longer, saying, "I shouldn't have this fear. Something is wrong with me," I noticed it and released it.

Instead of continuing to ask yourself any of the negative "what ifs" listed above, change what you say to yourself. Say, "I am willing to show up in the face of fear, and trust that I have this dream for a reason. I've figured things out before, and this is figure-outable, too."

Instead of going into a downward spiral, admit, "I have the fear of success, but I'm not alone. Christine has it. Her clients have it. I'm calling this fear out and I'm going to start telling a different story and stop letting it block me, TODAY."

2. Make a Clear Plan

The second thing I did - and I want you to do this too - was I realized the times when I didn't have a clear plan, were nearly always because fear was blocking me in some way.

Unfortunately, just telling yourself, "Get over it!" doesn't usually work. At least not overnight. Just like everything else you've been working on to grow your business, changing your mindset takes time, dedication, and repetition.

And the best strategy is simply to get started on it! And since belief in yourself is critical to your success, that's the reason I work with my clients both on business strategy and on mindset, right from the beginning.

No, it's not the glitzy, magical, catchy-but-also-totally-untrue "make money overnight while you sleep" promise. But it's REAL, and it's sustainable, and it turns you into the person you want to be along the way.

3. Reach Out For Help

Stop telling yourself, "I should know how to beat this already, on my own, and for free." Most people *don't* do it on their own... for free... Most truly successful people pay a mentor or coach to help them build a business.

The fear of success has the potential to continue to control you as long as you allow it to. It's going to prevent you from reaching your goals and being the very best version of yourself you can be. Overcoming it requires MORE than just talking about it to yourself. You need to find a way to hire someone to help you get over this hump.

Here's what one of my own amazing clients shared with her community about moving through her fear of success:

> I have a coach who has gone through all these
> emotions and feelings with me. She gets it! I feel

supported and she has helped me realize that my holding back is not of service to anyone, especially my tribe, my community, my family and society in general. She brought to light how the consequences of me holding myself back from success are far more profound and painful.

It's Your Turn Now. It's Time to Overcome Your Fear... of Success and Failure

Delegate or Die

Why do women so often feel like we have to do it all? We can - and must - learn to delegate and outsource, starting with the stuff we hate!

Sara Blakely, the founder of Spanx and the youngest self-made female billionaire, is not her own CEO! Why? Because she doesn't want to be!

Her biggest piece of advice for business owners: "Hire out your weaknesses as soon as you can afford to."

A woman in my community turned down a huge growth opportunity for her business because she wanted to make sure she was present for her family.

I asked her, "Why can't you have people handle the parts of your business that you don't like? You've done the hard part of creating your brand and offerings; why do you have to be the one physically doing every piece of the business?

You don't have to do that. You can hire that out and just do the parts of your business you enjoy, still be present for your family, and make more money than you do right now, because you're trying to do everything and finding yourself stressed out about every little thing."

See the difference? It, like so much of what we've discussed in this book, is a mindset shift!

Above all, remember: Today and every day to come, you can do this!

WHERE TO GO FROM HERE

W ell, there you have it: the path to replacing your income, doing what you love, and making great money doing it, from wherever you choose to be in the world.

It's based on the *7-Step Income Replacement Formula:*

1. Decision
2. Mindset
3. Niche
4. Offer
5. Marketing
6. Visibility
7. Sales

And within Mindset - which is sooo important! - we looked at:

- Why it's so important
- Money mindset stories
- Conquering fear and self-doubt
- Developing confidence and consistency

I encourage you to go back and re-read the chapters where you know you need to do some work, and do the exercises I've included as well. When you do that, you'll be well on your way to leaving your "9 to 5"!

Before you go though, here's what I want you to remember on this journey:

You have complete permission to:

1. GET AND STAY MOTIVATED THAT THIS IS POSSIBLE FOR YOU, TOO

It's not just for the women whose stories you've read on these pages.

The only difference between them and you is that they followed the formula you've just learned in this book. They showed up in spite of their fears and doubts and they took one simple step at a time.

2. SUCCEED ON YOUR OWN TERMS, NO MATTER WHAT YOU'VE BEEN TOLD OR WHAT YOU'VE BELIEVED IN THE PAST

However quirky or weird or "unrealistic" your business idea or your passions seem, I guarantee you that someone has made a boatload of money doing something weirder - like making a killing in an online business teaching cat grooming (Seriously. True story).

3. DREAM, AND DREAM BIG!

Dreaming IS practical! Dreaming, when followed with inspired, aligned action, helps you figure out exactly what you want, so you can go and get it!

4. ASK FOR HELP TO GET THERE

Contrary to pervasive high-achievers' beliefs, asking for help is NOT a weakness. Asking for help is key to resilience, consistency and persistence, all of which are crucial to your business-building journey.

Remember that your first steps for help can be found over at lifewithpassion.com/bookbonus, which I've designed specifically to help you take everything you've learned in these pages to the next level.

Follow the steps. Revisit this book again and again to help you get what you need, when you need it. Do the work, stay the course, and you will succeed.

I leave you with one final simple strategy: make a commitment and decide right now what your next step is. What are you going to do in the next 24 hours to move you one step closer to replacing your income? Write it down in your workbook in big bold letters. Schedule the time to do it on your calendar. And act.

Then let me know what you decided! I'm so excited to hear what you did and to celebrate it with you, no matter how big or small, so be sure to share it with me and the Life With Passion community in my Facebook group.

Lots of love,

Christine

ABOUT
THE AUTHOR

Christine McAlister is the founder of Life With Passion, a company that helps high-achieving, motivated entrepreneurs use their unique gifts to quit and stay out of their "9 to 5" jobs by building a business they love.

In her varied professional career, Christine has been a professor and career counselor, and founded companies in marketing, agriculture, and household products. Most important though, she always knew she wanted to be an entrepreneur, and started her first business on the side of a job that was sucking the life out of her every day. When she quit her job, Christine replaced that income within the first month.

After a few entrepreneurial ventures, when Christine experienced the worst tragedy a parent can imagine, she realized that she needed to allow herself to do and be *more...* It was soon after that life-changing event when Christine started her fourth company by identifying her Zone of Genius, and smashing through fear, self-doubt, and obstacles that had been holding her back from sharing her true gifts with the world.

All these experiences helped Christine "crack the code" on business success, and she developed a simple 7-step formula to share with other high-achieving entrepreneurs. Those who work with Christine are also quitting their "9 to 5" jobs and staying out, building online businesses out of their passions.

Christine is a mom, wife, and horse-loving, dog-rescuing entrepreneur who lives in Kentucky with her husband, daughter, and rescue animals. She wants to help you do what you love, replace your income, and quit *your* job!

Ready to smash through your obstacles and create your own success story?
Want to know how you can work with Christine?
Grab your exclusive book bonuses at

LifeWithPassion.com/bookbonus

or email

info@lifewithpassion.com!

88568951R00125

Made in the USA
Lexington, KY
13 May 2018